TABLE OF CONTENTS

INTRODUCTION

"Only the dead have seen the end of war." (Plato)

The current United States war paradigm tends to focus on swift rather than decisive victories. Operation Iraq Freedom (OIF) witnessed "catastrophic success" – the rapid disintegration of coordinated Iraqi conventional military resistance – during major combat operations. (Franks et al, 2004) However, over two years later insurgent forces are still conducting coordinated small unit operations in Iraq against coalition forces. The insurgent forces' will to continue to resist remains unbroken. Ironically, the United States' focus on swift victories may have enabled what would have been a limited resistance movement to fester into a large scale insurgency. Quick victories are the effect of a consequence adverse approach to warfare. Although these quick victories are publicly popular, and therefore politically desired, they hinder the United States' military's ability to apply overwhelming, or decisive, combat power for the duration of operations and set the conditions for the continuation of hostilities by threat insurgent forces. Quick victories are not bloodless and may actually increase the number of casualties over time.

Following the fall of Baghdad, the insurgents, also known as anti-Iraqi forces (AIF), did not view themselves as defeated, or even facing defeat, even after the United States led the coalition to unprecedented results after twenty-one days of the "shock and awe" campaign in March and April of 2003. Therefore, they retained their will to conduct irregular warfare against coalition forces, the Iraqi military and security forces. Later these attacks expanded to include both the local Iraqi populous and infrastructure. Consequently, the will of the populous in the United States, as well as in other coalition countries, will increasingly deteriorate as the situation changes from both tactical and operational success to strategic stalemate.

Why did the United States military fail to exploit its ability to win the war to also win the peace? The answer is strategic and operational mismatch resulting in the culmination of the operations prior to decisively defeating the insurgents. Winning the war is operational. Winning the peace is strategic. Victory is determined by strategic success, not operational and tactical success. The combatant commanders' challenge is to nest operational objectives with strategic objectives against competing demands both nationally and internationally. These competing demands may restrict the means, decisive military forces, required to properly achieve the desired objectives.

The combatant commander is responsible for winning the war at the operational level. Additionally, the combatant commander or joint force commander, by default, is also responsible for winning the peace, a strategic objective. War is messy and things get broken. Other government organizations do not have the capabilities or the desire to put the pieces back together. Civilian agencies are not organized, trained or prepared to rebuild, restructure and restart a nation. Therefore, it is the United States military who, by default, is charged with putting things back together. Water and electric services must be restored, looting halted, and daily life resumed by the local populous. The military demonstrated this capability in rebuilding Germany and Japan after the United Stated defeated them in World War II.

The linchpin in winning the war and winning the peace is the continuous application of decisive force across all phases of an operation. This also forms the basis for successful conflict termination. Successful conflict termination translates into conditions that are favorable to the United States. It does not mean the military forces come home after seizing the enemy's capital while the ink is still drying on any agreements. In fact, it means the opposite. Conditions favorable to the United States can only be created when the enemy is convinced it cannot prevail.

This translates into a lack of will. Breaking the will of the enemy requires decisive force throughout major combat operations and stability and support operations. No one ever won a war by being kind to enemy combatants during a war. The combatant commander brings the enemy to the negotiation table by defeating or neutralizing an adversary's fielded military forces or operational center(s) of gravity.

Joint Publication (JP) 1-02, Department of Defense Dictionary of Military and Associated Terms, defines center of gravity as, "Those characteristics, capabilities, or sources of power from which a military force derives its freedom of action, physical strength, or will to fight." (Joint Staff et al, 2004) Dr. Joseph Strange, a leading authority on centers of gravity, is more definitive when he contends the enemy's center of gravity at the operational and tactical level is inherently a specified enemy military force or unit. (Strange, n.d.) Conversely, the combatant commander's friendly operational center of gravity, what he must protect, is the apportioned military forces he tasks organizes to apply combat power against the enemy's fielded military forces. Strategic centers of gravity are political leaders, governments or a strong-willed population. (Ibid)

The combatant commander determines what operational military strategy best accomplishes the military objectives required to support national objectives. These national objectives are either limited, (e.g., restore territorial boundaries as in Operation Desert Storm (ODS) or unlimited (e.g. regime change as in OIF). This paper will demonstrate that during a conflict joint force commanders must apply a military strategy of annihilation at the operational level. A military strategy of annihilation at the operational level applies decisive force throughout the duration of military operations to support national objectives. Furthermore, such a military strategy at the operational level both sets the conditions for successful transition from major combat operations to stability and support operations, and, more importantly, enables the combatant commander to pierce the cognitive domain of the adversary, thus impacting the strategic level of war and securing the United States' national objectives.

However, the combatant commander must overcome not only the enemy, but also political and fiscal constraints, an over-reliance on technology, and an extremely casualty adverse culture. These challenges work to frustrate the combatant commanders' ability to employ a military strategy of annihilation during both the decisive phase of operations and the transition phase of operations. The force that is decisive during major combat operations is not necessarily a decisive force during stability and support operations. The decisive force's center of gravity may change as the enemy's strategic and operational centers of gravity change.

Regime change and the application of a military strategy of annihilation are specifically identified in doctrinal publication and rooted in American history. *Marine Corps Doctrinal Publication (MCDP) 1-1* advocates the prudent application a military strategy of annihilation to unlimited objectives as well as limited objectives. Two examples of successful regime change and the application of a military strategy of annihilation are exemplified in the restoration of the Union during the American Civil War and the "unconditional surrender" of the Axis Powers in World War II. The history of the United States also contains several failed regime changes. The most recent example, but on a smaller scale, is Operation Restore Hope in Somalia in 1994. The United States failed to match national objectives and military strategy during Operation Restore Hope resulting in the application of an insufficient friendly center of gravity to successfully accomplish the national objectives as they continued to evolve.

The success of regime change in Iraq is still undetermined. The United States has been in Afghanistan since October 2001 and has been in Iraq since March 2003. The American Civil

War lasted four years and was followed by another twelve years of reconstruction. The United States conducted combat operations in multiple theaters in World War II for four years followed by the occupation of Berlin and Tokyo. The United States, fueled by the Cold War which lasted forty-six years from 1945 to 1991, still has military forces stationed in Berlin and other German cities, as well as Japan – sixty years later. The Global War on Terrorism (GWOT) began October 7, 2001. The United States will not reach the forty-six year mark in the GWOT until 2047 and the sixty year mark until 2061.

To win the GWOT requires a strategy of annihilation. This paper will propose a new definition for the term military strategy of annihilation. In the process of developing a definition for the term strategy of annihilation it will employ the following methodology: examine the nesting of national and military strategies; discuss the opposition to a strategy of annihilation; examine centers of gravity; discuss General Ulysses S. Grant's campaign during 1864 – 1865 to win the American Civil War as a case study for the successful application of an military strategy of annihilation; address the relationship among casualty aversion, the search for technological silver bullets and force structure; and identify lessons learned. The United States military must be prepared to conduct a war of annihilation to secure national objectives and provide for America's security.

Grand National Strategy

> "The higher level of grand strategy [is] that of conducting war with the far-sighted regard to the state of the peace that will follow." (Sir Basil Henry Liddel-Hart)

America's military is subordinate to America's elected civilian leadership. Therefore, military strategy is subordinate to national strategy. America's civilian or political leadership directs the employment of the military to support national objectives. "War," as Clausewitz said, "is merely a continuation of policy by other means." (Clausewitz et al, 1993) War employs all the elements of national power – diplomatic, informational, military and economic (DIME). This paper is focused on the military instrument of national power at the operational level. It is important to understand the relationship among the three levels of warfare: strategic, operational and tactical. War is fought on multiple levels. It is important to win them all.

Since March 2005 the United States publishes three strategic capstone documents: the *National Security Strategy of The United States of America (NSS)*; the *National Defense Strategy of The United States of America (NDS)*; and the *National Military Strategy of the United States of America (NMS)*. Currently, only the *NSS* and the *NMS* are required by law. Regardless, the *NDS* is an official Department of Defense document, and, therefore, is official policy for the United States.

Strategy by definition is integrated or coherent. The *NMS* is derived from the *NDS*, one level up, and the *NSS*, two levels up. The related proponents for these documents are the Chairman of the Joint Chiefs of Staff, the Secretary of Defense, and the President of the United Sates. These strategic documents articulate the ends (desired objectives), ways (proposed courses of action or assigned tasks) and means (available national resources) of the United States' overall strategy at each level. At the national level, just as at the operational or tactical level, it is imperative for subordinates, in this case the combatant commander, to understand the intent of the higher level leadership one and two levels up.

The *NSS* identifies the strategic intent and outlines the strategic goals on the United States. The *NDS* establishes overarching defense objectives to guide the *NMS*. (*National Military Strategy of the United States of America*, 2004) The *NMS* outlines how the armed forces will implement the *NDS's* overarching objective to support the *NSS's* objectives in both peace and war. It is through the application of military force, or threat of its application, that the *NMS* influences the behavior of nation states and other international actors. Since 9/11, it has specifically targeted transnational actors such as terrorist groups, as well as nation states, as an audience.

The aim of the current *NSS* and the objectives of all the documents, although less ambiguous than previous administrations, is still very broad. The current *NSS* (2002) aims to, "[h]elp make the world not just safer, but better." It is unambiguous in that it states the United States in making the world better, makes no distinction between terrorists or extremist organizations and those who support terrorists, and reserves the right to employ a doctrine of preemption. However, it is also broad in that it does not specifically map out how we will achieve our objectives. Collectively, these two qualities work together to deter and dissuade potential adversaries from threatening the United States' interests.

The *NSS* seeks to achieve the objectives of the United States by applying the elements of national power to influence nation states and transnational actors. The objectives of the current *NSS* are:

- Political and economic freedom;
- Peaceful relations with other states; and
- Respect for human dignity.

The NDS's objectives complement those of the *NSS* by focusing on how the military, the only element of national power the Secretary of Defense and the Department of Defense can directly influence, can support national strategic objectives. The current *NDS* objectives (2005) are:

- Secure the United States from direct attack;
- Secure strategic access and retain global freedom of action;
- Strengthen alliances and partnerships; and
- Establish favorable security conditions.

The current *NMS* objective's (2004) are:

- Protect the United States against external attacks and aggression;
- Prevent conflict and surprise attack; and
- Prevail against adversaries.

The *NMS* is nested within the *NSS* and the *NDS* and enables the joint force commander to exercise initiative within intent to best translate objectives into military action. These actions are the plans and operations required to orchestrate military campaigns designed to secure national objectives. Therefore, military strategy is an extension of national strategy.

The current *NSS* has been called a grand strategy. For clarification, grand national strategy will be used hereafter to distinguish national strategy from international or coalition grand strategy. According to Professor John Gaddis, a renowned Cold War historian, the current *NSS* is one of only three grand national strategies in the history of the United States. The other two grand national strategies were the United States' national policies under President John Quincy Adams following the War of 1812, and those of President Franklin Roosevelt following the attack on Pearl Harbor. (Gaddis et al, 2004)

Gaddis cites three common characteristics of grand national strategies. First, grand national strategies are generated by crisis on American territory. The War of 1812 witnessed the British invasion of the capital and subsequent burning of the White House in 1814, while the

Japanese attacks on Pearl Harbor sunk five American battleships and killed 2,400 servicemen. The events of 9/11 resulted in the deaths of over 3000 people and served as the catalyst for the current *NSS*.

Second, grand national strategies are comprehensive and consistent in that they treat all adversaries and regions the same. President Adams sought to expand the United States by eliminating Spanish, French, English and Russian territorial claims. President Roosevelt sought unconditional surrender of both Germany and Japan. The current grand national strategy makes no distinction between terrorists and those who harbor them.

Third, grand national strategies have both short-term and long-term objectives. (Gaddis, 2003) President Adams sought to secure the security of the United States through territorial expansion and using pioneers to settle new territory before foreign powers could claim the land. (Gaddis et al, 2004) President Roosevelt's plan, implemented and further developed by his successors, sought to expand American security by spreading democratic governments and building free market economies to make the world better following World War II. Just as was the case with the previous two grand national strategies, the current one looks beyond the current administration's term in office in its aim to make the world better and safer for future generations of Americans.

The current *NSS* also reserves the right of the United States to exercise the doctrine of preemption – the right to apply any combination or all the elements of national power in self-defense against an imminent threat. Only when all the elements of national power are fully committed to breaking the will of our adversaries can the nation prevail at the strategic level.

The reality of the new security environment, characterized by the emerging threat of transnational actors and extremist organizations opposed to the United States, limits America's ability to apply all the elements of national power and threatens the traditional understanding of security. Extremist organizations do not provide a diplomatic medium through which to create a political dialogue. These organizations are both non-nodal and transnational making them difficult to directly target with economic sanctions and/or informational campaigns. Extremist organizations are by definition extreme. These organizations have an acquisition-to-use timeline approach towards weapons of mass destruction. Extremist organizations need only to acquire weapons of mass destruction in order to employ them. Lastly, extremist organizations have repeatedly demonstrated they do not regard human life, either of others or their own, the same way as Americans.

These dynamics significantly impact the ability of the United States to effectively leverage the non-military elements of national power against these organizations and force its leadership to rethink the traditional understanding of deterrence. Extremist organizations and their supporters must be addressed directly.

War, or the commitment of military forces to armed conflict, should be a last resort. Only after the United States determines its national objectives, whether limited or unlimited, cannot be achieved through a preponderance of diplomatic, informational and economic means should the United States focus on the military element of national power as the primary means to achieve objectives. When that path is chosen, the mission of the armed forces of the United States must be to win its wars. In the absence or marginalization of the other elements of national power, America's military must be employed decisively to have the credibility to deter threats to the United States' national security and vital interests. The degree of credibility must be that much higher to deter groups bent on the destruction of America at the expense of their own lives.

When the military element of national power is applied to achieve unlimited political objectives, power vacuums may be created due the elimination of foreign national political leadership. The United States must be prepared to fill these vacuums with a commitment to create security conditions conducive to favorable regional and international order; a commitment that is planning, resource, and troop intensive. These requisite capabilities are only found in the military; therefore, by default the military assumes the lead role for nation building. However, as mentioned earlier, the decisive military force applied during major combat operations to win the war does not necessarily translate into a decisive military force capable of winning the peace following the post hostility phase. At the operational level, strike aircraft, tanks, bombers, and cruise missiles are capable of destroying the enemy's fielded forces, eliminating command and control nodes, and even decapitating strategic adversary leadership targets. However, only large numbers of troops on the ground are capable of winning the peace.

The combatant commander operates at both the strategic and operational level of war. *JP 1-02* defines the strategic level of war as, "the level of war at which a nation, often as a member of a group of nations, determines national or multinational (alliance or coalition) security objectives and guidance, and develops and uses national resources to accomplish these objectives." (Joint Staff et al, 2004) The operational level of war is defined as

> The level of war at which campaigns and major operations are planned, conducted, and sustained to accomplish strategic objectives within theaters or other operational areas. Activities at this level link tactics and strategy by establishing operational objectives needed to accomplish the strategic objectives, sequencing events to achieve the operational objectives, initiating actions, and applying resources to bring about and sustain these events. (Ibid)

For example, one of the strategic military objectives during OIF was regime change. (Franks et al, 2004) One of the supporting operational objectives was to seize Baghdad. The seizing of Baghdad required tactical engagements to secure the Baghdad airport and key crossing sites in and around the city. Seizing Baghdad, an operational objective, is the link between regime change, the strategic objective, and securing the Baghdad airport and key crossing sites in Baghdad, tactical objectives.

Sun Tzu and Clausewitz are two of the most well known and quoted military theorists in history and remain relevant today. It is commonly held that Sun Tzu, whose theory of war is rooted in Eastern thought, and Clausewitz, whose theory of war is founded in Western thought, are focused on different levels of strategy and methods of war. Sun Tzu is seen as the practitioner of the indirect strategic approach, advancing the maxim it is best to win without fighting. Clausewitz is viewed as advocating the direct approach at the operational level by focusing on the destruction of the enemy's fielded forces. However, as with all theories, they are best applicable when combined together rather than treated as stand alone prescriptions for conducting warfare. Combing the two theories reveals that they are nested rather than on opposite ends of the spectrum. Specifically, it is the willingness to apply overwhelming military force at the operational level to decisively destroy an adversary's military forces that creates the credibility to impose one's will and generates the strategic capability to win future conflicts without fighting.

The United States military must apply a strategy of annihilation at the operational level in order to achieve strategic victory against the insurgent forces in Iraq. A military strategy of annihilation sets the conditions for the simultaneous application of the elements of national power both regionally and globally. A grand national strategy, the ends, requires a grand strategy at the levels below it, the ways, to be successful. An unambiguous commitment to the consistent application of decisive military force supports an unambiguous grand national strategy committed to the preservation of the United States' vital interests. A grand military strategy at the operational level is an extension of a grand national strategy. Annihilation, properly understood and applied, is a grand military strategy.

Military Strategy of Annihilation

"History does not long entrust the care of freedom to the weak or the timid."
- Dwight D. Eisenhower (BrainyQuotes)

Responsible political leadership should never take the prudent application of military forces off the table as an option to achieve national objectives and/or to protect the vital interests on the nation. Similarly, responsible military leadership should never take a commitment to decisive or overwhelming military force off the table to accomplish those same national objectives and the protection of those same vital interests.

JP 1-02 does not introduce the concept of a strategy of annihilation into the joint military lexicon. The term annihilation has a very negative perception in today's politically correct society and progressive modern military establishment. The reason for this negative stigma is two-fold. First, a strategy of annihilation conveys a wanton application of military force. Second, the term annihilation tends to be confused with the term attrition. The key is clarification in terms of both concept and terminology.

JP 1-02 defines attrition as "the reduction of the effectiveness of a force caused by loss of personnel and materiel." (Joint Staff, et al, 2004) There is neither a joint definition for a strategy of annihilation nor a joint definition for a strategy of attrition. However, *MCDP 1-1* describes a strategy of annihilation as seeking to eliminate the enemy's ability to resist, thus leaving him unable to oppose the imposition of the aggressor's will. (USMC Combat Development Command, 1997)

MCDP 1-1 refrains from using the term attrition. In lieu of attrition, it addresses a strategy of erosion. *MCDP 1-1* asserts a strategy of erosion is employed when military objectives are limited and the United States seeks only to raise the enemy's costs so high that the enemy will find ending the conflict more attractive than continuing to fight. (Ibid)

Erosion is used as a euphemism for attrition. Why not a strategy of attrition? The word attrition is fixed in the American psyche as a protracted conflict, or long-term commitment, a quagmire, with images of significant casualty numbers on both sides. Currently, Islamic extremist organizations are waging a strategic war of attrition against the United States in Iraq and around the world. The United States, as a democratic society, is at a disadvantage in such wars since the government derives its power from the consent of the governed. The government cannot be divorced from popular sentiment or it will be replaced by a new elected government who is perceived to be sympathetic to the sensitivities of the voting majority. Therefore, a protracted conflict can lead to the populous demanding withdrawal before the strategic or operational objectives are achieved.

Strategies of attrition are typically applied by weaker states against stronger states as demonstrated by the North Vietnamese during the Vietnam War. A commander employing an attrition strategy has a negative aim of wearing down an enemy before his own forces reach their own culmination point. The culmination point is the point at which a military force can no longer effectively conduct operations, either offensive or defensive, due to insufficient resources and time in relation to their objective. Clausewitz described the culmination point as the point in time when "…the remaining strength is just enough to maintain a defense and wait for peace." (Vego, 2000) Culmination points occur at the tactical, operational, and strategic level of war. The strategic culmination point in a war occurs only once. (Ibid)

A military strategy of annihilation is perceived as the total physical destruction of the enemy since military forces are the main effort and the adversary's military forces are the main object of such a strategy. Annihilation is more than killing and breaking things to win the war of wills, or influencing the enemy's behavior and that of potential enemies. The description of annihilation in *MCDP 1-1* focuses on eliminating the enemy's will to resist, not merely his physical military forces. The physical destruction, or threat, of all or part of the enemy's fielded military forces may not be necessary to eliminate the enemy's will to resist. For example, the Wehrmacht was strategically defeated at the end of World War II even though the German Army still possessed large numbers of armed forces. (USMC Combat Development Command, 1997) The American and Allied forces had consistently demonstrated a willingness to confront and defeat all the German armies, ravaged by over four years of war, between them and their objectives. The German political will was broken as epitomized by Adolph Hitler taking his own life.

A strategy of annihilation is also incorrectly associated only with total war in which combat is not restricted to force on force engagements on well-defined battlefields, but also involves the widespread killing of noncombatants, destruction of resources and critical infrastructure. However, an operational or military strategy of annihilation focuses on the ends; the deliberate killing of combatants as well as the necessary destruction of resources and facilities with an understanding they must later be rebuilt.

As stated in the introduction, a strategy of annihilation at the operational level was employed during both ODS, to secure limited national objectives, and OIF, to secure unlimited national objectives. Annihilation strategy should be incorporated into joint doctrine and terminology and defined as:

> A military strategy which applies decisive joint force, capability and sustainment to eliminate the enemy's will to continue hostilities through the continuous application of combat power across the spectrum of military operations throughout the depth of the battlespace in order to degrade or destroy the essential conditions or resource requirements the enemy needs to resist friendly forces in order to achieve both limited and unlimited national objectives.

A joint force commander applying an annihilation strategy retains a positive aim in that he seeks to defeat the enemy well before reaching his forces' own culmination point. Operational victories employing a strategy of attrition are short-term, while operational victories applying a military strategy of annihilation are decisive since they enable the joint force commander to retain the capability to exploit operational success over the long-term.

Role of Annihilation Strategy in Asymmetric Warfare

"It is wise in war not to underrate your opponent. It is equally important to understand his methods, and how his mind works." (Hart et al, 1991)

Asymmetry is perceived as a strategy employed by a less industrial and/or militarily weaker adversary against a more industrial and/or militarily capable enemy. For example, during the Vietnam War, the North Vietnamese had a comparative advantage of popular and political will compared to the South Vietnamese and the United States. The word asymmetry, much like quagmire, has become a word that inspires fear and doubt in the minds of Americans. As early as 1997 the *Quadrennial Defense Review Report (QDR)* stated, "U.S. dominance in the conventional military arena may encourage adversaries to use . . . asymmetric means to attack our forces and interests overseas and Americans at home."

American political and military leadership continues to define asymmetry one way – against the United States. Joint doctrine predominantly limits its discussion of asymmetry to *JP 3-11* and *3-12,* framing the concept of asymmetry in terms of nuclear, biological and chemical (NBC) employment against the United States. (Joint Staff et al, 1995 and 1993) The current Depart of Defense advocates a capabilities based approach to warfare and force structure. The 2001 *QDR* states capabilities based approach to warfare "requires identifying capabilities that U.S. military forces will need to deter and defeat adversaries who will rely on surprise, deception, and asymmetric warfare to achieve their objectives." (2001)

Capabilities based warfare is not new. All warfare is capabilities based. Militaries cannot apply weapons or technology they do not possess. The section in the *QDR* on a capabilities based approach states the United States seeks to develop a comparative advantage by applying a capability against the enemy's strategy for which the enemy does not have or is not prepared to defeat. Properly interpreted, the United States seeks to apply asymmetric warfare against its adversaries.

Asymmetry properly understood is neutral. Asymmetry can be employed by both weak and strong states. Asymmetry is not a method of warfare exclusively reserved for less developed states, or transnational actors, to apply against more developed states or conventional forces. Asymmetry is leveraging comparative advantage. Comparative advantage is when one has a different or greater capability, whether slight or significant, in a specific area. Asymmetry is also employing off-the-shelf technology in an outside the box methodology such as using large airplanes as weapons of mass destruction in large population centers. The concept of asymmetry has been practiced throughout the history of warfare. It is the mark of a great strategist and a prudent commander. Asymmetry does not seek to create a level playing field; it seeks to keep the opponent off balance and unable to concentrate strength of effort.

The United States possesses a comparative advantage militarily in leadership, organization, training and equipment. These advantages translate into a more lethal and adaptive force. A force when properly applied, supported and resourced is decisive across the spectrum of military operations. A military strategy of annihilation seeks to conduct asymmetric warfare against adversaries by capitalizing on comparative advantages. The United States sought to employ an asymmetric approach to warfare against the Soviet Union during the Cold War at the operational level by applying qualitative advantage against Soviet quantitative advantage. This was the basis for the Army's Air, Land Battle concept which served as the bedrock for doctrine from the 1980's through the early 1990's.

Asymmetry first appeared in joint doctrine in 1995 in *JP 1, Joint Warfare of the Armed Forces of the United States*. (Metz, 2001) Additionally, *JP 3-0, Doctrine for Joint Operations* and later the *Joint Doctrine Encyclopedia*, 1995 and1997 respectively, presented a simplified concept of asymmetry with limited utility. The doctrine described asymmetric engagements restricted to dissimilar forces such as land and aerial or maritime and aerial. (Ibid) The focus on asymmetry is based on specific service components not on comparative advantages which form the basis for asymmetric warfare.

The current *QDR* and prominent analysts hold the United States' adversaries will seek a strategy of attrition due to the United States military's dominant capability on the conventional battlefield. When confronted with a strategy of attrition there are three options: 1) Avoid conflict and encourage further aggression by an adversary in the future by demonstrating a lack of will; 2) Employ a similar strategy of attrition against the adversary and engage in a long-term war of wills; or 3) Apply a strategy of annihilation to dictate where and when the enemy will be subjugated to another's will. Option three is the prudent choice. Therefore, America's military must be empowered to match its dominant warfighting capability with an indomitable commitment to eradicate the United States' enemies to discourage its adversaries from pursuing a strategy of attrition, or any other asymmetric means, against the United States. This is the new deterrence paradigm.

Ultimately, forces and resources are limited and physical realities dictate military commanders must selectively apply economy of force and prioritize efforts throughout the battlespace to sustain operations. Insufficient troops-to-task and resources can escalate risk to an unacceptable level as the operational situation evolves. Under a military strategy of annihilation the joint force commander is afforded operational flexibility through sufficient military capability and resources to redirect forces and reallocate combat power to assume operational risk, but not an to the point where it becomes operational gamble. A risk is an action whose probability and consequence of failure is not decisive at the operational level. A gamble is an action whose probability and consequence of loss results in failure at the operational level. Joint task force commanders may manage risk by planning for the employment of reserves or combat multipliers to influence or reverse the current tide of battle either at the point of attack or to support the economy of force effort. Reserves and combat multipliers must be readily available to effectively manage risks.

In Iraq, and other countries ruled by authoritarian regimes, the lessons learned in OIF to date can be applied. Iraq, despite the recent success of the elections, remains a country split along cultural and religious fault lines. The Kurds, the Sunnis and Shiites are all opposed to each other. Open source intelligence reports and regional experts believe that Iraq may ultimately be divided into three distinct areas or separate countries and/or have a civil war in the not too distant future. A civil war could lead to one or multiple failed states which could further destabilize the current situation and subsequently provide a sanctuary for extremist organizations.

The groups in Iraq have always been divided over territorial claims and religious tenants. However, under Saddam Hussein these groups did not openly seek independence or threaten civil war. The reason is these people, to include the current insurgent force regardless of regional ethnicity, understand power. It is part of their culture and something that was lost on the United States in its initial efforts to create a free and self-determining Iraq after the removal of Saddam's regime. This can partially be attributed to the assumptions incorporated into the planning process for OIF.

In the planning process assumptions are used in lieu of facts to determine enemy capabilities or reactions to United States' actions. Assumptions must be definable, measurable and quantifiable. Energy and resources must be applied to determine the veracity of an assumption, especially when success or failure of a plan depends on that assumption being valid. Specifically, in OIF the assumption discounting the requirement for significant land forces to exploit initial success, address unforeseen events, or rotate forward combat forces was not valid. (Collins, 2003)

This assumption failed to appreciate the significance of the Sunni population, the former power base, compromising thirty-two percent of the Iraqi population. The country of Iraq has a population of 25.4 million. (Iraq, 2005) This equates to a Sunni population base of 8.1 million from which to form a potential resistance against American military forces. In fact, eighty percent of all attacks against United States and Coalition forces occur in the Sunni-dominated area of central Iraq, the Sunni Triangle. (Pike, 2005) The assumption that the Sunni would quietly accept defeat resulted in employing a decisive force during major combat operations which was an insufficient force for stability and support operations.

The United States, and other countries committed to putting an end to extremism, must make the thought of victory, or even tactical success, against the United States and its coalition partners a remote possibility. A firm commitment to employ lethal and decisive force at the tactical and operational levels will serve as the first step to stemming the tide of extremists at all levels by placing fear and doubt in their minds. Additionally, such a firm commitment supported by overwhelming forces will sustain momentum as military forces transition from major combat operations to the reestablishment of local law enforcement and social normalcy at the operational level. This will set the conditions for social and political reform.

Large numbers of infantrymen patrolling the streets set the conditions for security. Large numbers of infantryman, supported by armored vehicles, moving unopposed through the streets are a visible physical force. Military forces must not only be highly visible, significant in number, but must be aggressive. These visual cues communicate to the local population that the United States, not the insurgency, is in control of the battlespace.

An article in the New York Times captures this well when describing the transition of responsibilities for northern Baghdad from the 11,000 man Marine force to the 1,200 man Army force. The article reads:

> The departure of the marines came as something of a shock in this shattered capital. The roughly [11,000] troops of the First Marine Division had been a highly visible and forceful presence, mounting foot patrols through the streets, working with neighborhood committees to stop looting and arson, and running a civil affairs effort to help get the police, hospitals, electrical and water service up and running... The soldiers of the Army's Third Infantry Division, who have now spread out to cover the city, have struck a lower profile. (New York Times, 2003)

The Army's much smaller force had a degraded capability of projecting presence and was limited to securing key facilities and road intersections. The Army was able to address some of the security concerns in the area; however, the Army's forces could not adequately confront potential combat operations in the streets, and could not sustain the community connector initiatives instituted by the Marines. Stability operations are in large part about solving people's problems and human interaction. Thus, these operations require boots on the ground.

Land forces are the main effort during stability and support operations. Therefore, they are the occupying force's operational center of gravity. They are the force that offers resistance against insurgent operations. Conversely, an insufficient number of troops on the ground will fail to convince insurgent forces, and the local population, the insurgents are fighting a loosing battle. Also, as a secondary effect, an insufficient commitment of troops on the ground may fail to discourage new recruits from joining the insurgents efforts and sustain passive support if the local population perceives the possibility of insurgent victory as plausible. These dynamics enable the insurgent forces to expand their operational center of gravity.

Centers of Gravity

"It is my design, if the enemy keeps quiet and allows me to take the initiative in the spring campaign, to work all parts of the army together, and somewhat toward a common center." - General Ulysses S. Grant describing his intent for his campaign in 1864 (Grant et al, 1990)

The above is an excerpt from General Grant's intent issued to General Sherman in April 1864 for the upcoming Union offensive campaign against the Confederate forces. The five-pronged attack established a ring around the Confederate capital and brought the weight of the Union army on top of the Confederacy. Whether by genius, or even chance, was General Grant referring to both the Confederacy's strategic and operational centers of gravity? Did General Grant mean, "[W]ork all parts of the army together, and somewhat toward a common center [of gravity]"?

Centers of gravity, whether strategic or operational, are the primary source of resistance when an adversary seeks to impose its will on an opponent. (Strange et al, 1998) Failure to properly identify centers of gravity may result in an inability to secure objectives at the least cost, or even failure. An inability to minimize the expense of blood and treasure in a democratic government results in a loss of popular support and potentially strategic defeat. The Vietnam War provides an example of this phenomenon.

A common misplaced perception among the American public throughout history is that an enemy's capital is the enemy's strategic center of gravity. This perception, and the motivation for revenge, explains why the American public has historically been willing to endure high casualties en route to an enemy's capital. This misperception continues today. COL Killebrew (USA, retired) contends, "The conventional attack into Baghdad and other Iraqi cities…however brilliantly executed, in retrospect looks like a strategy out of the 19th century-seize the enemy's capitol and the nation falls into one's hands like a ripe fruit." (Killebrew,

2005) It is not the enemy's capital that is strategic, but rather what is potentially in the enemy's capital – the strategic center of gravity. Strategic centers of gravity may be a political leader or party, or a moral force such as a strong will. Therefore, strategic centers of gravity can be difficult to target directly due to international protocol, political restraints, or a lack of physical quality.

As stated earlier, the center of gravity at the operational level is the enemy's military forces. Specifically, the operational center of gravity is a single identified military unit from the fielded military forces. This will usually be the main effort force in a given operation. Dr. Strange points out that the joint definition misses the mark on centers of gravity since it defines it as the source of power, or capability, for a military force, rather than the military force itself. Dr. Strange further expands on operational centers of gravity by describing them as something physical which can offer resistance by striking hammer blows against an enemy. (Strange, n.d.) Physical centers of gravity require a concentration of mass or of military forces. The greater the concentration of mass the stronger the operational center of gravity and the heavier the hammer to strike blows against the adversary's operational center of gravity. Conversely, the greater a friendly operational center of gravity's mass, the greater its ability to absorb blows delivered against it by the enemy's forces.

As a general rule, there is only one center of gravity at both the strategic and operational levels of war. Centers of gravity may be difficult to attack directly; however, if they are physical, they can be targeted, directly or indirectly, by striking blows. The question is not whether or not to attack centers of gravity, but how to attack them. A discussion of centers of gravity and its related components will help eliminate frequent misunderstandings about centers of gravity and develop a systemic approach for determining how to best deliver effective strikes against a strategic or physical centers of gravity.

Centers of gravity are linked by critical capabilities and critical requirements to critical vulnerabilities. (Strange et al, 1998) This is commonly expressed as Center of Gravity – Critical Capabilities – Critical Requirements – Critical Vulnerabilities, or CG – CC – CR – CV. For example, assume an enemy's operational center of gravity is its main effort for an attack – the 33rd armor brigade. This is the unit that will strike hammer blows against the opposing defense. Critical Capabilities are the abilities (e.g. shoot, move and communicate) which enable a center of gravity to deliver strikes against an adversaries center of gravity. Critical Requirements are the conditions or resources (e.g. ammunition and fuel) required to achieve or sustain a critical capability. Critical Vulnerabilities are critical requirements (e.g. fuel depots) vulnerable to attack whose destruction will erode a center of gravities ability to achieve a critical capability. Critical vulnerabilities should be the focus of combat operations.

This method also works for strategic centers of gravity lacking physical quality such as a population with a strong will. CCs and CRs for this type of center of gravity still have a physical dimension. Therefore, strategic centers of gravity may be targeted indirectly.

Further analysis on the relationships between a center of gravity and its components is best understood when shown as hierarchical rather than linear. The CG – CC – CR – CV hierarchical model is illustrated below:

GENERAL

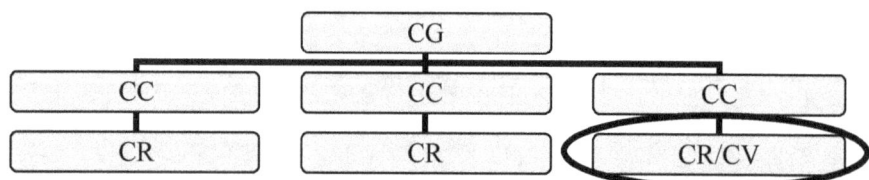

SPECIFIC

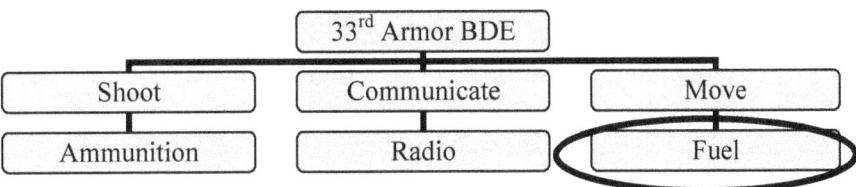

Wars are no longer won in a single engagement or decisive battle as during the height of the Napoleonic Era of warfare. A single major joint operation, such as Operation Just Cause in 1989 to remove Manuel Noriega from power in Panama, is not the norm to secure national objectives. Just as there are no technological silver bullets, there are no operational silver bullets. Strong strikes will not necessarily be decisive by themselves, but must be coordinated with other strikes across tactical and operational actions. Current combat operations require multiple joint military operations to secure national objectives. This is more so when those national objectives are unlimited. Therefore, "…final success can only be achieved by focusing on a combination of vulnerable critical requirements that can be neutralized, interdicted, or attacked simultaneously or sequentially" toward a common center of gravity. (Strange, n.d.) This is done through campaign planning.

Campaign plans translate a combatant commander's strategy by linking multiple joint military operations within a given space and time to secure both strategic and operational objectives. (Joint Staff et al, 2004) Campaign planning, the process of developing campaign plans, is the nexus between operational art and the operational level of war. Operational art integrates the employment of military forces at all levels of war to achieve strategic and operational objectives. (Ibid)

In planning the campaign it is important to remember the moral and physical limits of military power. There are limits on using military power to secure long-term or strategic objectives. Military power is limited by proportionality. It is necessary to be as brutal at the tactical and operational level as the circumstances require, but not more. (Kaplan et al, 2002) Tough actions at the tactical and operational level, when tempered by sound judgment, provide "credibility to make peace" from a position of power. (Ibid)

Dr. Strange lists three considerations to the physical limits of military power. First, the right force in terms of capabilities and size must be employed. Do not send an artillery battalion to do the job of an infantry division. Second, military forces must be sustained and cannot be properly supported once they exceed the operational reach of logistics. Extended operations over time and space require planned consolidation and reorganization, or operational pauses. Third, the cumulative effect of combat actions, casualties, terrain and weather, climate, extended lines of communication and human limits contribute to culmination short of victory, the point of no return, when strategic, operational and tactical considerations are not nested, regardless of early operational and tactical success. (Strange et al, 1998) An insufficient operational center of gravity relative to an adversary's forces ultimately results in military defeat. Military commanders and planners must apply the same systemic approach in identifying their own centers of gravity. Failure to properly identify and protect one's own strategic and operational centers of gravity may also result in defeat.

Centers of gravity have a dynamic quality in that they can change. The enemy's strategic and operational centers of gravity, and their related components, during major combat operations will not necessarily be the same as the strategic and operational centers of gravity during support and stability operations. There are two reasons centers of gravity change. First, the nature of the conflict may change. Second, the objectives of the conflict or mission may be altered. These two considerations may or may not be related.

An example of the nature of a conflict changing occurs when military forces shift from major combat operations to stability and support operations such as Coalition forces did in both Afghanistan and Iraq following OEF and OIF. In this example the changing of the center of gravity and the changing of objectives were related.

Stability and support operations may not always follow major combat operations, but may be conducted by themselves, in which case it the stability and support operations are the decisive operations. An example of this is Operation Provide Comfort between December of 1992 and March of 1994 in Somalia. Initially the Coalition's objectives were to provide humanitarian assistance; however, the Coalition, which included the United States, expanded its objectives to include disarming the local warlords. This change in the operational objective had the unintended effect of changing the operational center of gravity from a starving populous to armed clans of gunmen. Because the enemy's operational center of gravity changed, the Coalition's operational center of gravity, forces designed to support humanitarian operations, exceeded their physical limit. Additionally, the United States' strategic center of gravity, popular support, was neutralized when the American public became confused about what the United States was doing in Somalia following the deaths of 18 military Service members on 3 and 4 October 1993.

The Iraqi strategic and operational centers of gravity also changed during OIF. Prior to and during major combat operations the strategic center of gravity was Saddam Hussein's regime. Later, during stability and support operations the strategic center of gravity became the Iraqi people's will. The Iraqi Republican Guard, the Iraqi operational center of gravity during ODS, was not the same force in 2003 it was in 1991. In retrospect, the operational center of gravity during major combat operations may have been the Fedayeen Saddam, Saddam's Men of

Sacrifice. (Strange, n.d.) However, the tendency of victorious armies to fight the last war and gravitate towards their operational comfort zone, conventional combat in the case of America's military, ultimately results in poor planning.

It was the Fedayeen Saddam that protected Saddam's regime in Baghdad, not the Republican Guard. The Fedayeen Saddam was in Baghdad, as well as other Iraqi cities, where they could both intimidate the local population and attack extended Coalition supply lines. (Ibid) They stood between Coalition forces and Saddam Hussein's regime. This is not the enemy the United States war gamed against. Consequently, the Fedayeen Saddam remained intact after major combat operations and formed the core of the resistance movement during the initial stability and support operations. The resistance movement should have been anticipated given the American military occupation. However, the United States was unable to exploit its initial "catastrophic success" and lost the initiative because the decisive force that seized Baghdad was not a decisive stabilization force.

When the United States surrendered the initiative it gave the resistance and other groups in the region time to organize and develop into a large scale insurgency. The AIF, estimated at 40,000 strong benefits from a support network of more than 200,000 people providing intelligence, logistics and sanctuary according to Iraqi intelligence service. (Pike, 2005) United States analysts estimate the insurgency's peak active fighting strength at around 20,000 between July and December of 2004. American troop strength in Iraq ranged from 140,000 to 148,000 and other coalition forces ranged between 22,000 and 25,000 over that same period. (O'Hanlon, 2005) The United States Army operates on approximately a 1:7 tooth-to-tail ratio, and assuming a uniform distribution across all services of this ratio for the purposes of simplification, this equates to 18,500 American combat forces. This is less than the United States analysts' estimate of 20,000 insurgents, with no tooth-to-tail ratio, available to conduct operations against friendly forces.

Correctly identifying the center of gravity for stability and support operations, the transition phase, is just as critical to success as it is during major combat operations, the decisive phase. The end of major combat operations is not the termination of operations. It is during the transition phase that conflict termination is accomplished by directly addressing the enemy's strategic center of gravity as well as the changing operational center of gravity. Therefore, campaign plans must establish links between securing objectives at the operational level and defeating the moral center of gravity at the strategic level. (Strange, n.d.)

To establish these links requires vision on the part of the joint force commander. When the objective is regime change, he must anticipate if and when the strategic center of gravity will shift from the former regime to a strong-willed population. Only a strong-willed population is capable of being a strategic or moral center of gravity; otherwise they will not offer resistance and, by definition, will not be a center of gravity. (Ibid) This same vision requires the joint force commander to employ his military forces in such a manner that the enemy's population knows they have been defeated. The joint force commander, acting within the Law of Armed Conflict and supporting rules of engagement, must not be inhibited by enemy casualty counts or collateral damage. The enemy's forces must be made to feel the "agony of war" and the masses must be witness to the United States armed forces commitment to apply controlled violence to impose its will on those who oppose it through armed engagements. (Peters, 2005) Only through such deliberate execution of combat operations can operational objectives be secured and exploited to secure long-term stability. Failure to do so results in only a temporary termination of the current war or conflict "…if the spirit of the resistance still burns in the hearts of" an enemy's population. (Strange et al, 1998)

Grant's Grand Campaign

"Military necessity admits of all direct destruction of life or limb of armed enemies, and of other persons whose destruction is incidentally unavoidable in the armed contests of the war." General Orders Number 100, Instructions for the government of Armies of the United States in the field by President Lincoln, April 24, 1863. (Lincoln, 1863.)

The first three years of the American Civil War was a war of attrition. The Confederate States of America (CSA) predominately employed a strategic defense, or war of attrition, while the Union forces of the North struggled to effectively prosecute the war and carry the fight to the Confederacy. Despite a vast superiority, or comparative advantage, in resources, manpower and industry, the North could not decisively defeat the outmanned and outresourced Confederacy until General Grant directed the Union Army toward a common objective – the Confederate fielded military forces – over time and space. General Ulysses S. Grant's offensive campaign from 1864 through 1865 is arguably the first example of a strategy of annihilation in a major conflict in American military history.

President Lincoln's issuing of General Order Number 100 illustrates his strong desire to not only defeat the Confederacy, but his frustration at not being able to win the war quickly. The strategic objective of the North was to restore the Union, or the regime change of the Confederacy. President Lincoln knew the survival of the Union, as well as his own political survival, depended on sustaining Northern popular support and winning the war decisively. He roughly laid out his national grand strategy to win the war within General Order Number 100 by outlining the Confederacy's strategic and operational centers of gravity: the strong-willed Southern population supporting the CSA and the Confederate Armies. Victory would require the elimination of popular support for Southern succession and the destruction of the Confederate Armies, specifically the Army of Northern Virginia commanded by General Lee. President Lincoln's challenge was, has it had been throughout the American Civil War, to find a military commander who could affect both the strategic and operational levels of war by applying a military strategy that was an extension of the President Lincoln's national strategy. The solution was found with the appointment of General Grant as the [combatant] commander of all Union forces.

General Grant employed land and naval forces, constant maneuver and significant reserves to apply continuous pressure throughout a non-linear theater of operations to deny the Confederate forces sanctuary and resources while systematically destroying their fielded military forces. He provided his subordinates adequate troops to tasks and an execution-centric approach that empowered his subordinates to use initiative within the commander's intent by emphasizing the purpose to be accomplished rather than a specified task. General Grant's conduct of warfare at the operational level to achieve strategic objectives is an enduring example of the successful deliberate application of an annihilation strategy.

General Grant's predecessors had failed to achieve decisive results and carry the war to the Southern states. Generals Halleck, McClellan, Hooker and Meade all saw battle as an end in itself, rather than as a means to advance an overall military strategy. General McClellan sought to prosecute the war while inflicting minimal damage to life and property in hopes of minimizing any bitterness between the North and the South at the end of the war. However, the Confederacy could not be defeated through a method of maneuver and minimal destructiveness. (Weigley et al, 1973) Such a strategy would spell doom for preserving the Union. General Meade's unwillingness to pursue General Lee following the Battle of Gettysburg may have lost an opportunity to exploit his initial success and hasten the end of the American Civil War.

Gettysburg proved to be a strategic turning point in the war. Given the Confederacy's smaller population base, the 28,000 casualties suffered at Gettysburg marked a culmination point short of victory for the Southern states. The operational center of gravity of the Army of Northern Virginia started down a glide path of combat power erosion from which it would not recover. The defeat at Gettysburg in July 1863 marked the beginning of the end for the Confederacy. However, that end could not realized by the Union through unrelated single engagements spread over several months.

In contrast to his predecessors, General Grant saw each battle, regardless of outcome, as a series of actions all connected toward achieving a common operational objective. (Ibid) It was not battles he sought to win, it was the war. Furthermore, Grant was firm in what he called a "conviction that no peace could be had that would be stable and conducive to the happiness of the people, both North and South, until the military power of the rebellion was entirely broken." (Grant et al, 1990) General Grant focused his efforts in the Eastern Theater on the Confederacy's operational center of gravity: the Army of Northern Virginia. General Grant focused the efforts of General Sherman in the Western Theater on the Confederacy's strategic center of gravity: the strong-willed southern population.

Consider the Confederate strategic and operational centers of gravity (COGs) identified in the following construct as the framework for General Grant's great campaign:

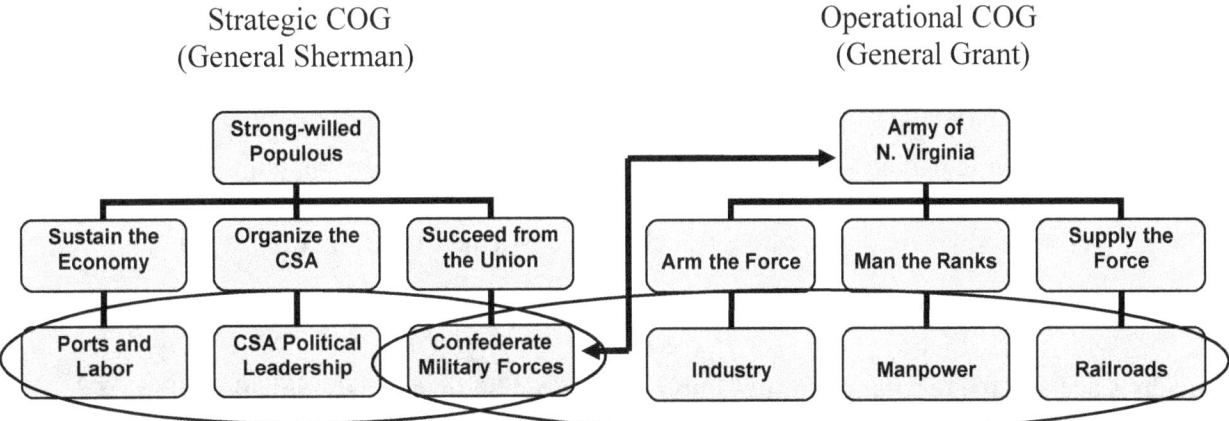

Grant sought to devise a grand campaign that would employ the principles of joint operations, objective, offensive and mass, to remove not only the Army of Northern Virginia but all the Confederate Armies from the battlefield. His general concept of the operation employed "…active and continuous operations of all the troops that could be brought to the field…to hammer continuously against the armed force of the enemy and his resources." (Ibid) Specifically, General Grant employed a simultaneous five-pronged offensive on the Eastern and Western theaters beginning in May 1864. (See Map A)

A two-pronged attack was conducted in the West and formed the Union supporting effort. General Sherman, the Western Theater commander, seized Atlanta and Savannah, two intermediate operational objectives, and threatened the rear operations of the Confederacy. General Grant instructed him to "…move against [CSA General] Johnston's army, to break it up, and to go into the interior of the enemy's country as far as he could, inflicting all the damage he could upon their war resources." (Ibid) General Sherman was supported by a joint Army-Navy operation under the command of General Banks to isolate "…the last functioning Confederate seaport," Mobile, Alabama. (USMC Combat Development Command, 1997) Keeping with his theme to put every soldier possible into the field, Grant instructed General Banks to strip his various headquarters down to the minimum in order to field a force of 25,000 – 30,000 for the expedition. (Griess et al, 2002) During the conduct of the operations in the Western Theater General Sherman remarked, "We are not only fighting hostile armies, but a hostile people, and must make old and young, rich and poor, feel the heavy hand of war, as well as the organized armies." (Weigley et al, 1973) General Sherman focused on the strategic center of gravity. He made peace and the restoration of the Union a better option than the continuation of the war.

A three-pronged attack was the foundation for operations in the East. The Union main effort, commanded by General Meade, with General Grant co-located, threatened Richmond from the North and had the task to destroy General Lee's Army of Northern Virginia. General Grant outlined General Meade's purpose when he instructed him, "Lee's army would be his objective point; that wherever Lee went he would go also." (Grant et al, 1990) General Butler conducted an amphibious landing and supported General Meade by threatening Richmond from the south to prevent the Confederates from concentrating forces against the main effort. (Griess et al, 2002) General Sigel conducted a supporting operation in the Shenandoah Valley to destroy war resources and prevent the Confederate forces from reinforcing from the north against the Union main effort. (Ibid)

In both theaters, General Grant gave his subordinate commanders a wide range of latitude by his emphasis on purpose and not task, or an execution-centric approach. Furthermore, his emphasis on putting every available soldier in the field not only expanded the Union's collective operational center of gravity, but also provided his subordinates further flexibility by giving them sufficient troops-to-task in order to react to the dynamics of chance and overcome friction.

Underlying General Grant's plan was his desire to leverage the industrial based North's comparative, or asymmetrical, advantage in manpower and resources against the agrarian based South. During the American Civil War the Union's peak military strength was 1,000,000 while the Confederates peak military strength was 600,000. (Wiegley et al, 1973) General Grant began his great campaign with roughly a 2:1 force ratio advantage to leverage against the Confederate Army. The North's tremendous population base advantage could supply an unmatched stream of replacement forces. In addition, the North contained 109,000 plants for the production of war resources and miscellaneous goods with 22,000 miles of integrated railway.

By comparison the South had 31,000 plants for the production of war resources and goods with 9,000 miles of non-uniform railways. (Rascon) Not only could General Grant field a larger army, but he could supply it and transport it faster as well.

The Union main effort's initial operations in the East met with stalemate in the Wilderness Campaign and the Battle of Spotsylvania while both supporting efforts in the East were also unsuccessful. General Grant, remaining focused on his objective, was undaunted and continued his offensive movement south toward Richmond to keep constant pressure on General Lee's Army of Northern Virginia. General Grant remarked, "Our success over General Lee's army is already insured." (Griess et al, 2002) Perhaps he sensed General Lee's army had reached the culminating point short of victory.

At Cold Harbor the action again settled into a stalemate, and again General Grant, focused on the war and not the battle, sought to keep the pressure on the Confederates by shifting his efforts on Petersburg, a critical rail center where the Union opened siege lines. Although losses on both sides were heavy, the key was reinforcements. The Union was able to reinforce its lines with 40,000 men and keep its end strength around 100,000, while the Confederates, with limited manpower and other Confederate forces fixed by General Sherman in the West, added just 24,000. (Ibid) General Grant's constant movement kept the shrinking Confederate Army committed to protecting Richmond thus forcing them to continually extend their defensive lines and denied them the full advantage of a prepared defense. Collectively these actions kept the Confederate forces from threatening Washington, thus protecting the Union's strategic center of gravity, President Lincoln. Additionally, General Grant's refusal to yield the initiative and superior capability to replace Northern losses protected the Union's operational center of gravity, the Army of the Potomac, by eliminating any windows of opportunity for General Lee in which he could effectively mass his own forces and counterattack. (See Map B)

General Sherman commenced operations in the West with a 2.5:1 force ratio advantage against General Johnston. The expansion of the war into the interior of the Confederacy had begun. General Sherman's deep penetration into Georgia exposed the Confederates' war resources, critical vulnerabilities, to his advance but it also extended Sherman's lines of communication and exposed them to attack. Following the successful Union action at Cassville, General Sherman cut his lines of communication. (Ibid) This enabled him to increase his rate of advance and minimize his force's vulnerability to Confederate action against the Union rear while increasing the weight of forces available to strike heavy blows against the Confederate forces as he continued to move south toward Atlanta, a key industrial site and transit point for war supplies in the center of the Confederacy. Though subsequent engagements en route were not decisive, General Sherman, like General Grant, remained focused on his intermediate operational objective, knowing no single battle would decide the outcome.

General Sherman conducted a siege of Atlanta. He systematically began cutting the rail lines out of Atlanta which supported the Confederate forces in the field. In late August, General Sherman shifted forces from securing his rear to weight his attacks on Confederate rail lines. (Ibid) Sherman's constant effort to increase the Union's striking power proved decisive when Atlanta fell in early September. The news filled the Northern populous with euphoria and all but guaranteed President Lincoln would be reelected. Also, the Union forces captured Mobile and its seaport, effectively freezing the South's ability to receive supplies or export goods for sale.

After destroying the production factories and remaining railroads in and around Atlanta, General Sherman, with his advantage in men and material, retasked himself to seize the initiative and commenced his March to the Sea in November 1864 to further cripple the war resources of the South. General Sherman's march was a "shock and awe" campaign in that it demonstrated the Confederate Army's inability to protect the population and, perhaps more importantly, the Union's ability to take the war to the entire South. (Ibid) His numerical advantage enabled him to divide his army in two to both address the Confederate Army of Tennessee to the north and further expand the war south into the heart of the Confederacy. He dispatched 30,000 men in the defense of Nashville against the Confederate Army of Tennessee. He then divided his remaining 62,000 man army for the March to the Sea into a left and right wing to expedite the march and reduce the foraging requirements. The Union advance covered a 60-mile-wide front and threatened the Confederacy along multiple axes. Once again cutting loose from his supply lines to increase his operational force (by approximately 15,000), he embarked on a campaign to deny the Confederate forces material and moral support. (Ibid)

General Sherman next seized Milledgeville, Georgia's state capital, and followed up his unopposed advance by marching his army through the streets to further psychologically disarm the Southern population. As General Sherman's army approached Savannah, the defending Confederate forces, realizing they would be defeated, withdrew rather than engage the Union. The Union force occupied the city on December 21, 1864. (See Map C)

In contrast to movement which characterized General Sherman's March to the Sea, the Eastern Theater had become one of two sieges, one against Richmond and the other against Petersburg. General Grant's immediate objective was to cut the railroads into the cities and force General Lee from the safety of the trenches, at which point General Grant would apply his overwhelming superiority of numbers to crush the Confederate Army. (Ibid) Initially General Grant tried to sever the railroads through a series of cavalry raids. However, he soon determined that "…only by planting an infantry force firmly astride the railroad could the flow of supplies be stemmed." (Ibid) Eventually the Union lines stretched 37 miles which thinned the defending Confederate forces and made them vulnerable to attack. To further increase his numerical advantage, General Grant brought in artillerymen assigned to the defense of Washington and made them infantrymen as he sought to achieve the right size force with the right capabilities. General Grant instructed his corps and division commanders to attack in the absence of further orders when the time was right. (Ibid)

General Lee sought to regain the initiative on March 25, 1865 by attacking the Union flank and forcing General Grant to shorten his occupied trench lines. Although the attack achieved total surprise, the Union's overwhelming numerical advantage enabled it to quickly blunt the attack. On April 1, the Northern forces captured Five Forks thus constricting the Confederates escape routes to the west. General Grant then pressed the Union advantage, conducting a successful attack the next morning against Petersburg and making the Confederate position no longer defendable. General Lee began to withdraw forces from Petersburg and Richmond that same night. (Ibid) General Grant immediately began to pursue the Confederate Army. On April 3, 1865 the Union forces occupied Richmond.

The Union forces were able to press the retreating Confederates from both the front and the rear which enabled them to get inside the Confederates decision cycle causing the withdrawal to become uncoordinated and resulting in the capture of General Lee's rear guard and supply trains on April 6. The Confederate forces of 30,000 had been cut in half. (Ibid) On April 9, 1865 General Lee surrendered and for all intent and purposes the American Civil War was over. The Confederacy's operational center of gravity was defeated.

It is important to understand how the Union forces in the two theaters worked together. General Grant's efforts in the East may seem less impressive when compared to General Sherman's exploits in the West; however, it was the action in the East that greatly contributed to General Sherman's success. General Grant fixed the Army of Northern Virginia, the South's operational center of gravity, in the East and prevented those Confederate forces from disrupting General Sherman's campaign against the strong-willed southern population, the South's strategic center of gravity.

The Union supporting effort, still led by General Sherman, began its march into the Carolinas in January of 1865 and continued to destroy war resources and carried the war to those who supported the Confederacy. General Sherman's intent was to work his way north and link up with General Grant and the Army of the Potomac, the Union main effort, to destroy the Army of Northern Virginia, the primary operational objective. All parts of the Union's military worked towards a common center. Furthermore, General Sherman's forces continued to expand from 60,000 during the siege of Atlanta to over 88,000 during the campaign in the Carolinas. (Sherman et al, 2000) The fate of the Confederacy was sealed. General Sherman accepted the surrender of General Johnston on April 26, 1865 thus ending the campaign in the West.

The Union employed political, informational and military elements of national power to defeat the Confederacy. The attacks against the Confederacy's manpower and labor, the Confederacy critical vulnerabilities, illustrate how these elements were woven together. President Lincoln issued the Emancipation Proclamation in 1863 seeking to deprive the South of slave labor. General Grant's grand military campaign inflicted casualties and captured prisoners. Additionally, General Grant quit exchanging prisoners to further limit the capability of the South to man its armies. For all casualties the ratio of Confederate to Union losses was 1:1.3.

However, the Union held a 2.5:1 advantage in population base (23 million versus 9 million). Since the Confederacy's population included 3.5 million slaves, the Union's advantage was closer to 4.2:1; to the Confederacy, the loss of each soldier was more critical than the loss of a soldier was to the Union. (Weigley et al, 1973)

During General Sherman's operations in Georgia, and the Carolinas the following year, Black laborers began to gravitate toward the Union armies, leaving untended farms and plantations. Furthermore, General Sherman's movements in the heart of the South compelled Confederate soldiers to desert and return home to protect family and property. (Ibid) Lastly, General Sherman's operations dealt psychological blows to the Southern population as the very visible Union forces seemed to move wherever and whenever they wanted within the heart of the Confederacy. The final psychological blow was dealt when Union forces captured Jefferson Davis on May 10, 1865. (Griess et al, 2002)

General Grant demonstrated an uncanny ability to orchestrate multiple corps and division sized units across dual theaters and attack the enemy's fielded forces in depth; however, his operational brilliance was not an end in itself. The Union's comparative advantage, or asymmetry, in manpower and industrialization were present throughout the war, but this was not an end in itself either. It was General Grant's merging of resources with operational art that achieved a strategy of annihilation and preserved the Union. General Grant's deliberate application of a strategy of annihilation was exemplified in the Union's active maneuver, continuous offensive, and common focus on the campaign's objectives. This application was supported by a willingness to eliminate the South's economic and industrial capability as demonstrated by General Sherman's campaign in the West. General Sherman's deep penetration into the interior of the Confederacy exposed the South's critical vulnerabilities in depth to the Union forces and convinced the Southern people they were fighting a war they could not win.

It is important to note that the deep penetration into the South also made General Sherman's army vulnerable as the whole South became a non-contiguous battlefield. Securing the Union's lines of communication and garrisons during the March to the Sea would have reduced General Sherman's combat by power more than 40%. (Weigley, 1973) General Sherman recognized the threat to his forces and was able to task organize his sufficiently large force to sustain the momentum of the campaign to facilitate the end of the war. The challenges of executing military operations across extensive lines in space and time are not a new phenomenon in the conduct of war.

In the end, the Army of Northern Virginia was not only an operational center of gravity, but was also a strategic critical vulnerability. Although the Army of Northern Virginia was not totally annihilated, it ceased to be an effective combat force. Operational centers of gravity protect strategic centers by resisting an adversary's operational center of gravity. In the final days of the American Civil War the Army of Northern Virginia could only deliver glancing blows against the Union's operational center of gravity; it could no longer oppose the Union's forces on the battlefield. A military strategy of annihilation defeated the South when a strategy of attrition could not.

Casualty Aversion and Defining Military Effectiveness

"You know you never defeated us on the battlefield," said the American colonel. The North Vietnamese colonel pondered this remark a moment. "That may be so," he replied, "but it is also irrelevant." Conversation in Hanoi, April 1975 between Colonel Summers, Chief Negotiations Division, US Delegation, and Colonel Tu, Chief North Vietnamese Delegation. (Summers et al, 1984)

According to an official Depart of Defense report, 47,424 Service members were killed as a result of hostile action during the Vietnam War (Vietnam Conflict - Casualty Summary, 2004) and another 304,704 wounded in action. (Smith, 2000) Casualty data released by North Vietnam in April 1995 reported the North Vietnamese Army and the Viet Cong endured 1,100,000 killed during hostile action and another 600,000 wounded in action. (Ibid) For each American killed, twenty-three North Vietnamese soldiers/guerillas were killed, but the United States was unable to win the Vietnam War.

The reason the United States failed to win the war is that North Vietnam possessed a comparative advantage in political will and popular support on a scale of orders of magnitude greater than that of the United States' civilian leadership and population at large. As discussed earlier, democracies are at a disadvantage in a protracted war, or war of attrition. Since popularly elected civilian leadership is subject to removal from office in the next election, political leaders may be casualty adverse. (Klinger, 2002) In fact, data from a contracted Army study finds the "…propensity of democracies to win declines over time" while the ability of autocratic states does not. (Ibid)

After the fall of Baghdad the American populous seemed to ask, "Now what?" The tearing down of a statue of Saddam Hussein did not signal the end of the war, but rather the need to build a new Iraq. OIF entered the stability and support phase of the operation to set the conditions for nation building. As American servicemen and servicewomen continue to die on a daily basis, how does the military and the nation measure the effectiveness of stability operations or nation building?

Success in nation building is measured in economic and quality of life metrics such as the number of telephone and internet subscribers, ongoing water projects to support sanitation and health, average hours of electricity per day, unemployment rates, exchange students studying in the US, and, in a country like Iraq, how many million barrels per day (mbpd) of oil are produced. In the longer term the results of nation building can be measured in life expectancy and child mortality rates. These all require time and do not easily translate as a measure of military combat effectiveness to the American public at large and to a two-party political system, where ideologues will ask, "How many active phone circuits equal one military servicemember's life?" Stability and support operations are military operations. Therefore, the military will tend to find military metrics to communicate the effectiveness of conducting stability and support operations: the number of city blocks patrolled, total square kilometers secured, the number of weapons caches found, or tonnage of captured weapons destroyed.

Regardless of what metric the military attempts to use, the answer in the popular press invariably defaults to the number of deaths sustained during operations as the American population struggles to understand, and the media attempts to communicate, the continued accumulation of American lives. This is the case even though deaths are a better defined as measures of cost, not effectiveness. However, since the number of casualties determines the popular support, this metric will be used. Therefore, the question then becomes what casualty metric is to be employed to tabulate United States costs: total casualties killed relative to the total number of enemy killed; casualties killed and wounded per 100,000 serving in a combat theater; or combat related deaths per day of combat operations. This paper will employ combat deaths per day as a measure of cost to analyze both past conflicts and the current campaigns in Afghanistan and Iraq.

Winning the nation's wars means killing the enemy. Killing the enemy means exposing Service members to the enemy's observation, weapons engagement ranges, and possibly death. Earlier this paper stated a strategy of annihilation enables the combatant commander to pierce the veil of the enemy's cognitive domain to impact the strategic level. It is also important to look under the veil of the American psyche and glimpse into its cognitive domain at the impact of casualties on the United States' strategic and operational strategies. The average American interprets combat deaths, regardless of other metrics, as a sign the United States' military is in jeopardy of being defeated. Every additional casualty moves the military closer to defeat.

The American populous' excessive aversion to casualties contributes to the United States' over-reliance on technology by seeking to substitute electrons for deployed forces and combat power. There is a Newtonian effect. One of Newton's three laws of motion holds that for every action there is an opposite and equal reaction. Every Service member the United States does not deploy decreases the strength of the military forces' operational center of gravity and increases the adversary's perception that the United States is not committed to winning decisively. The cliché "perception is reality" is cliché because it's true. Somalia is an example of tactical defeat that resulted from an insufficient political involvement leading to a weak operational force on the ground. This tactical defeat had strategic implications which were not lost on America's adversaries who sought to pursue unconventional strategies to bloody America's nose. The events of 9/11 are a clear example of al Qaeda believing the United States would be intimidated and not seek action beyond lobbing a few cruise missiles against a non-nodal enemy. Al Qaeda apparently further believed the American people would not support a massive United States military response and, more importantly, would not support deploying thousands of Service members to the other side of the world to fight a potentially long drawn out conflict.

The challenge of sustaining the will of the populous while combat casualties accumulate during a protracted war is not new to American history. During the American Civil War the Union forces endured 110,100 killed in action, and the Confederate forces absorbed another 94,000 combat deaths which equates to 68.7 and 64.5 combat deaths per day respectively. (Faust, 2002) In fact, President Lincoln was in danger of loosing the election of 1864 prior to General Sherman capturing Atlanta and securing his reelection bid. Although the Northern forces were sustaining a greater number of casualties than the Confederate forces the Union was able to rally the public with decisive results by marching through the Southern states, delivering tangible results and relieving the pressure on the Union capital. These victories served to generate positive media coverage in the North which sustained the popular support of the Northern population. The Union's campaign in 1864 yielded the Confederate cities of Atlanta and Savannah which served as quantifiable measures of success or effectiveness. These measures of success were quantifiable because they could physically be counted or pointed to on a map. A secondary effect is that the Northern populous, despite continuing accumulation of casualties, came to accept combat fatalities as the cost of fighting a war.

In World War II the United States suffered 1.1 million casualties, of which 291,557 were battle deaths, averaging out to 213.6 per day. (Principle Wars in which the United States Participated, 2003) In addition to punishing the Japanese for the attack on Pearl Harbor and the Germans for declaring war on the United States, the American public was willing to sustain these high casualty rates for two reasons: to obtain revenge and because it could see progress in the march to Tokyo and Berlin.

ODS resulted in 147 deaths to United States Service members attributed to hostile action during forty-three days of combat, or 3.44 combat related deaths per day. (Persian Gulf War - Casualty Summary, 2004) The end state of the Operations Desert Storm was two-fold. First, the American public falsely learned that wars, regardless of objectives, could be won with less than one-hundred and fifty casualties and just four days of ground fighting. Second, the public came to believe precision guided bombs, not boots on the ground, were the key to victory. These two misperceptions, combined with the decline of the Soviet Union, were the basis for cutting the U.S. military nearly in half following the first Gulf War. The lesson lost was that Iraq's inability to counter the United States' overwhelming military capability kept Saddam Hussein from seizing the tactical initiative despite the Iraqi Army's superiority in numbers and arms early in the conflict.

The events of 9/11 momentarily steeled the will of the American people and stirred cries for justice. The government quickly linked the hijackers to the Taliban regime, Osama bin Laden, and the al Qaeda terrorist organization based in Afghanistan. Additionally, the international community, which had no significant on going economic or political ties to Afghanistan, rallied around the United States and its cause. The United States quickly defeated the forces in Afghanistan and began to rebuild Afghanistan while suffering far fewer casualties than experts had predicted. The United States did in a few weeks what the former Soviet Union could not do in ten years – it won a war in Afghanistan.

The United State then turned its attention to Iraq. However, the debate between the United States government and the media, both national and international, on a credible direct link between Saddam Hussein and terrorist organizations served to undermine American and international support for the war in Iraq. United Nations and international opposition were linked to political and economic ties to Iraq. Additionally, a false expectation was created for the American people, and possibly some government officials, during OEF. This time it was believed it was possible to displace a foreign regime with Special Forces on horseback, precision munitions, and the support of local warlords. However, Iraq is not Afghanistan. The OEF model does not apply to the OIF model.

OIF is a non-contiguous battlefield. The battlespace is not linear with clear delineation of front and rear boundaries and the disposition of friendly and enemy forces. The "shock and awe" offensive into Iraq, although extremely successful, further exacerbated the non-continguous dynamic. There was no clear separation between combat units, combat support and combat service support units, increasing the exposure of support units to combat. Support units consist of both male and female Service members. Consequently, twenty-four, or .033 per day, women have been killed by hostile action as of March 21, 2005. (Female Fatalities, 2005) The deaths of the female Service members have sparked a debate about whether of not the military is violating its policy to keep women from being exposed to combat. In ODS, five women were killed as a result of hostile action or .116 per day which is three and one-half times greater than that for OIF. (Female Personnel by Service, 1999)

As of March 19, 2005, OEF had resulted in 66 combat deaths. The metric for OEF is .052 casualties per day, or 1 combat death every 19.2 days. (Operations Enduring Freedom – Casualty Summary by Type, 2005) In fact, OEF is an afterthought for most Americans given its success as well as the subsequent lack of media coverage due to the fact that good news does not get ratings and the focus on OIF. The irony is that the American people were prepared to sustain a high threshold of casualties to strike back at al Qaeda and those who supported the terrorist organization in Afghanistan. Having established a clear link between al Qaeda and the Taliban the United States government did not need to exert great effort to energize the popular support of the American public for OEF.

Baghdad fell two years ago and the military is now challenged to provide quantifiable measures of its success to justify the continuing accumulation of US casualties and spending of tax dollars. According to Department of Defense statistics, the total number of American Service members killed by hostile fire as of March 19, 2005, two days short of two years after the start of OIF was initiated, was 1146, or 1.57 combat deaths per day. (Ibid) Desert Storm would have generated 2511 casualties over a two year period, more than double the current number in Iraq. The challenge is overcoming the aggregate number and the sustained drain on national resources and treasure as well as American blood.

On September 11, 2001, 3,020 people died in the attacks on the New York World Trade Center, the Pentagon and United Airlines flight #93. (World Trade Center New York Destruction) At the current rate it will require another three years and 100 days from March 19, 2005, for a total of five years and 98 days, before the deaths from hostile action in OIF equals 3,020. The challenge for the United States government is to communicate that it is strategically better to have three soldiers die every two days over several years in order to stem the tide of terrorism abroad by creating conditions favorable to freedom and self-determining governments than to have 3,000 Americans killed in a single day on American soil.

Minimization of casualties has become a cornerstone of sustaining popular support for military operations abroad while at the same time terrorists groups and insurgents wage a strategic war of attrition against America's military forces. Consequently, today's military is not risk adverse, it is consequence adverse. The military's leadership is not afraid to take risk. The military leadership is afraid of being the subject of a news story's talking points broadcast to millions of American homes about how the military got it wrong, or worse, wrong again. The power of the media to influence public opinion in opposition to military success was clearly demonstrated following Operation Just Cause. CNN and CBS ran split screens of President George H. W. Bush addressing the American public about the successful mission while also showing the flag draped coffins arriving at Dover Air Force Base, Delaware. (Rosenberg, 2003) This became known as the Dover Factor. The Dover Factor is the theory that Americans cannot maintain their support for war when such images of Soldiers, Sailors, Airmen and Marines are shown on television. Therefore, the media is banned from covering the arrival of America's fallen Service members. (Ibid)

The reality remains that decisions have consequences. When the United States makes a decision to commit military forces, whether it is major combat operations and/or operations on a smaller scale, it must also make a commitment to accept casualties. Attrition at the tactical level cannot be avoided when young men and women are sent into hostile environments. In the short-term the political leadership of the United States has the onus to prepare the American public for the realities of war. In the long-term, the political leadership coupled with the precedent established by an unwavering commitment to protect the United States' vital interests must continue to prepare Americans for the dark side of combat while also dissuading the enemies of the United States.

Think of war in terms of a sports analogy. Americans love a winner. In sports, fans love their teams. Fans love their teams more when they win games and championships. Its not enough to be up twenty-one to zero at halftime and then win twenty-four to twenty-two. Sports fans on the winning team will then focus on how and why their beloved sports team almost blew the game. Fans want their team to win the big game forty-two to three; forty-two to zero is better. The same is true of what America expects of its armed forces. The fathers and mothers, and increasingly the children and communities, of those who fill the ranks of the military services want a military that is beyond challenge and capable of winning decisively across the array of determined enemies and ambiguous threats.

The United States will remain at a disadvantage in wars measured in months rather than days in an environment characterized by the sensationalizing of the mainstream media, continuing confusion between measures of cost and effectiveness, and a focus on American casualties as the ends. National political leaders must assume the lead on communicating unambiguous national objectives to the American people and then properly employ the military forces assigned to securing those national objectives.

Impact of Combat Casualties on Recruiting

"The best way to honor our dead is to defeat the enemy." (Peters, 2002)

The decision to shift to an all volunteer force from a draftee organization in 1971 was a strategic decision to promote a professional military, as well as a political decision. The all volunteer force seeks to attract people who possess a sense personal commitment and patriotism while minimizing the potential outcries by the American public against military actions abroad. This shift coupled with time and military success has reduced large scale war opposition within the United States which was so prevalent during the Vietnam War period. In fact, during OEF and OIF military supporters often outnumber groups organized to oppose the war. However, only a small number of the all volunteer force comes knocking on the recruiters' doors. Therefore, military recruiters must reach out into the community to find the committed and patriotic individuals required to populate the ranks of the armed forces. However, a less than clear understanding by the American people of why military members are dying hinders recruiting efforts.

The United States' continuing force commitments in OEF and OIF, less than decisive results after the end of major combat operations in Iraq, and sustained casualty rates have adversely impacted the ability of the armed forces to meet end strength requirements to sustain the force. The perception for ordinary American citizen is the United States must not be winning because its forces are still deployed in large numbers, the Reserves and National Guard are mobilized and Service members keeping dying. This type of perception adversely affects popular support. During war it can be difficult to find volunteers without widespread popular support. The Army Reserve and National Guard recruiting efforts were the first components to feel the pinch of combat realities and shrinking nationalism as the events of 9/11 move further away in the past.

An analysis of OIF reveals the increasing demand on Army Reserve and Army National Guard forces. The Active to Reserve component mix has steadily increased. Across the total United States National Guard and Reserve force the demand has increased from 41,392 in October of 2001 to 170,066 in September of 2004; 83.5% of this number, 141,961, are members of the Army Reserve and the Army National Guard. (Project on Defense Alternatives, 2004) The demand OEF and OIF have placed on the Reserve force had greatly degraded the ability of the Army Reserve force to meet its responsibilities to support other OPLANS. The continuing strain on these Reserves prompted the Chief of the Army Reserve to conclude the Reserves are "...rapidly degenerating into a broken force." (Helmly, 2004) This is further reflected in the recent recruiting challenges incurred by the Army and Marines.

Air Force and Navy recruiters are turning potential new enlistees away while at the same time Marine Corps and Army recruiters are struggling to make their respective recruiting missions. The Army and Marine Corps, the land components, have sustained the most casualties during OIF. The total number of United States troops killed in Operation Iraqi Freedom went over 1,500 on March 2, 2005. The Army and the Marine Corps account for 97% of those killed. (Coalition Casualty Count: Metrics, 2005) The Navy and the Air Force account for 3% of Service members killed supporting Operation Iraqi Freedom. (Ibid)

The Marine Corps barely made their recruiting goals in November and December 2004 before missing their recruiting goal of 3,270 by eighty-four for January 2005. (Schmitt, 2005) It was the first time the Marine Corps did not meet a monthly recruiting mission since 1995, the same year it failed to meet its annual recruiting objective. (Ibid) In February, the Marines missed their recruiting goal of 2,964 by 192. (Kreisher, 2005) In March, the Marines fell fifty-six recruits short of their goal of 3,055. (Dunham, 2005) They remain 2% behind their recruiting goal for FY 2005. (*USA Today*, 2005)

The Army has been impacted especially hard. The Army Reserve failed to make its March recruiting mission by 46% and is 18% behind its year-to-date recruiting goal. (Ibid) The Army National Guard is 26% behind its year-to-date recruiting mission and has been short each month in FY05. The active duty Army fell 1,936 (27.5%) recruits short of its goal of 5,114 for February 2005 despite offering enlistment bonuses of $20,000 for a four year enlistment. (Moniz, 2005) It is the first time the Army has not achieved its monthly mission since May 2000. (Ibid) The recruiting shortfall trend continued in March with the Army missing its recruiting goal by 32% (Dunham, 2005); it is 15% behind for the current FY. (*USA Today*, 2005) There is evidence Army recruiters are cutting corners and bending the rules in an attempt make their enlistment mission. 320 substantiated incidents of recruiting improprieties occurred in 2004, up from 213 in 2002, the year before OIF. (Cave, 2005) This type of behavior undermines the credibility of the military's efforts to expand the force.

The military, specifically the Army and the Marines, cannot afford to have its credibility questioned when many Americans are already questioning the legitimacy of the regime change in Iraq. A lack of credibility and legitimacy creates tremendous friction to not only sustaining the current force, but the larger requirement to expand the force to meet the challenges of future conflicts. Efforts to sustain and expand the military are further frustrated by the continuing accumulation of American deaths in Afghanistan and Iraq.

There will always be attrition in war. The best efforts of to maximize force protection and minimize friendly casualties are ultimately limited by the chaotic and dangerous nature of war. Service members have been killed supporting campaigns in southwest Asia and more will continue to be wounded and killed in the pursuit of national interests. Combat casualties may occur in spikes. For example, the largest single incident in Operation Desert Storm was the death of twenty-eight Army reservists killed and another ninety-nine wounded when their barracks in Dhahran, Saudi Arabia was struck by an Iraqi Scud missile; this number represents 19% of the total killed by hostile action. (Defense Link News, 2001) In Somalia there were a total of 29 Service members killed. Task Force Ranger, a collection of Army Special Forces units, incurred 18 of the 29 combat deaths between 3 and 4 October 1993. (Selected Military Operations, 2003) Estimates on Somali combat deaths range from 500 to 1000, or a minimum of 27.7 Somalis killed for every Task Force Ranger member lost. (Knickerbocker, 2003) Overall the United States military casualty per day metric for Somalia was .25 per day. However, America's leadership, further burdened by unclear objectives in Somalia and a confused public who thought we were conducting humanitarian operations, responded to this single incident by halting aggressive operations and ultimately withdrawing American forces in Somalia.

As discussed earlier, this type of reaction encourages enemies of the United States to strike at America's military. Put simply, it is a formula for operational paralysis and strategic defeat. When a force stops to lick its wounds it ceases punishing its opponent. Striking the enemy harder at the tactical and operational levels following the deaths of Americans is the only correct response strategically (Peters, 2002) This means taking the gloves off, but it may also mean additional casualties. However, failure to strike back may mean more casualties in the long term whether through slow accumulation from road side bomb attacks, or another attack similar to 9/11 on American soil. "Combat deaths indicate that we are serious about destroying the enemy that we are willing to do whatever it takes," states LTC Ralph Peters (USA, retired), further adding, "I would be far more distrustful of a campaign without casualties." (Ibid)

This view seems counter-intuitive to the average American. However, it is the United States' commitment to put boots on the ground and employ those same boots in decisive combat tempered with a realistic understanding that incurring casualties is the cost of fighting wars, whether protracted or not, that wins the current war and deters others. America's leadership, regardless of the metric of effectiveness, must clearly communicate to the American public the strategic objectives supported by operational and tactical actions, and more importantly, the potential consequences of not securing those strategic objectives. An inability to do so will result in less than popular support from the American people and directly undermine the military's ability to fight and win on its terms as the combatant commander becomes encumbered by political considerations.

Less than popular support from the American people translates into a potentially insufficient recruiting pool for the military. The strategy of the United States to address the future security environment is determines the force-sizing construct to meet national objectives. The expanding of national objectives requires, as a minimum, a reevaluation of the force-sizing construct. Successful recruiting of the right people is paramount whether such an evaluation determines the current force structure will be sustained or expanded. Popular support, regardless of casualties, must be sustained if the military is to remain an effective force.

Over-reliance on Technology

"At the end of the most grandiose plans and strategies is a soldier walking point." (Stanton et al, 1985)

In the final analysis people kill people – not machines, not weapons not processes. Well trained and well disciplined Soldiers, Sailors, Marines and Airmen are the critical capability required for military forces to win wars. They are not the cornerstone of an effective military force, they are the foundation.

The desire to develop technological silver bullets is due to several factors. The first is America's aversion to casualties. Second, the United States faces the fiscal realities of training, manning, equipping and then deploying large forces. Third, Americans have an inherent distrust of large standing militaries inherent in democratic governments. Finally, Americans tend to trust technology. Consequently, and in conjunction with both the demise of the former Soviet Union and the wrong lessons learned during ODS, the United States' military has been reduced substantially, from 780,000 to 480,000 in the Army alone, while further reductions were still being considered until 9/11. The professional military establishment has responded by redefining the meaning of mass and firepower and moving towards a capabilities based force.

The United States' ascendancy as the world's preeminent military power and a dozen years of peace prior to 9/11 opened the door for think tank groups and corporate culture to push the military to focus more on acquisition and future force development rather than training the current force. These influences all seem to be focused on making the military more efficient. The challenge is efficiency does not equal effectiveness. The military's mission is to win the nation's wars, not its battles. Fighting and winning wars is complicated by the chaotic nature of the war, the element of chance, and free will. Effectiveness, not efficiency, is the realm of the military.

Technology is an enabler, and does not hold the answer to all the military's challenges. For example, the military continues to gravitate toward network centric warfare to enhance situational awareness and enable self-synchronizing units. Will this evolution provide commanders a near-perfect real-time picture of friendly and enemy operational centers of gravity? The short answer is no. There will always be challenges.

First, computer screens cannot replicate the fear, friction and fog permeating both friendly and enemy forces. In combat things become confused. Orders will be misinterpreted. Communications will fail at the wrong time. Leaders will rise and fall. The effects of sleep deprivation, the loss of a friend, and the threat of death at any moment may profoundly impact individual and group dynamics. All of these emanate from the fog of battle and work to create friction that must be overcome when confronted by an adaptable enemy exerting physical resistance. This information is not readily available to the eye in the sky.

Second, just because you can see the enemy does not mean you know the enemy. You do not know the enemy until you have fought him. Intelligent and resourceful enemies will anticipate U.S actions and employ deception and adaptive, or asymmetrical, methods to defeat U.S. technology and tactics.

Third, there is no such thing as perfect knowledge; therefore, chance encounters and unforeseen events will happen. In an urban environment it is impossible to know every door the enemy will hide behind and every street corner at which he will bury an improvised explosive device (IED). Technology, even when supplemented with other intelligence sources, will not provide a 100% solution. However, it enables units to lead with their fist and not their face when conducting operations. When punched they must still be prepared to punch back hard and effectively.

Technology has the potential to stifle initiative for two reasons. First, individuals may become overly dependent on a perception of perfect situational awareness, and loose the ability to apply professional judgment to fill information gaps. An inability to transition from the computer screen to the immediate battlespace to make timely decisions surrenders the initiative to the enemy. Second, individuals may become overly concerned with who is watching them on the big screen in the command center rather than executing within the commander's intent. Senior commanders need only cross this fine line between command and control once to establish a precedent that will cause subordinates to surrender the making decisions on employing forces and weapons systems during the next engagement. Subordinates will not always select the textbook solution or what the boss would have done, but that is irrelevant. The important thing is they make a decision, right or wrong, which enables them to have a fighting chance. The key is they have to keep fighting. Even a wrong decision can create momentum, action against the adversary and/or leadership confidence, which may be sustained to overcome the enemy.

Forces must be resourced properly to overcome battlefield dynamics and the chaos of war. The operational center of gravity is found in the concentration of mass. The wrong type of force creates and insufficient center of gravity, regardless of situational awareness and textbook solutions, and may be irrelevant against the enemy's center of gravity.

In addition to stifling initiative, technology's ability to gather and produce information may cause the user to get inside his own decision cycle, or Observation, Orientation, Decision, Action (OODA) loop. Communication systems were capable of transmitting sixty words per minute during World War II. This ability increased to 100 words per minute during the Vietnam War. (Myers, 2003) This is a 67% increase in capability over a 25 year period. During ODS communication systems were capable of relaying 200,000 words per minute and nearly 6,000,000 words per minute during operation OIF. (Ibid) This is a 290% increase in capability over a 12 year period.

Consider the above example about capability in the context of information and intelligence. Not all information is intelligence. Information must be analyzed before it becomes intelligence. Intelligence must be processed in a timely manner if it is to be actionable. Actionable intelligence is intelligence the joint force commander can use to influence the battlespace by getting inside the enemy's OODA loop. Although the amount of information is vast, the average adult only reads between 200 – 300 words per minute and thus the ability to determine actionable intelligence is minimized. The technologies now required are the tools that sort and prioritize information not to keep processing information faster. Actionable intelligence remains the one of the United State' toughest challenges today. Specifically, reliable human intelligence (HUMINT) is critical. HUMINT intelligence is derived from sources inside the enemy's organization or close to the source, thus providing increased opportunities to get inside the enemy's OODA loop.

Technology can erode comparative advantage by infecting militaries with the engineer's disease. Engineer's disease occurs when continually improving a superior, or proven, system, weapon or platform to the point it is counterproductive. An example of this is the German obsession with tanks during World War II. The Germans focused on continually improving the tank beginning with the standard Panzer followed by the Panther and Tiger class tanks. The tanks were continually equipped with heavier main guns and more armor than the Allied tanks, and were able to destroy multiple Allied tanks for every German tank lost. However, these tanks were also slower and consumed large quantities of fuel. Additionally, these tanks took longer to produce given the extended research and development phase and factory production requirements.

The cumulative effect of these dynamics was the inability of the Germans to produce tanks faster than the rate at which they were loosing tanks at the end of the war. Some German tanks were even produced without machine guns for self-defense in an effort to get them to the front faster, making them susceptible to infantry attacks. By the end of the war the over-engineered German tanks were regarded as strategic assets and limited in their employment across the battlespace. In contrast, the Russians developed the combat reliable T-34 tank and were able to mass produce them faster than they were losing tanks in battle; they were able to employ them in large numbers across the depth of the battlespace.

Not all technology is durable or supportable. If it breaks, it cannot be counted on when the bullets start flying. Operational and tactical actions cannot hinge on equipment that will not work in the rain or survive a combat roll. The more gadgets outside the existing supply and maintenance systems employed the greater the need for contractors to service these items further increasing the logistics tail.

The theme of transformation dominates discussion about how the United States will shape the joint military force of the future. Erroneously, technology has been identified as the point of spear to transform today's legacy threat-based force to tomorrow's objective capabilities based force. This is further demonstrated in the shift in continuing education allocation and priorities of the United States military officers. For example, the Army has dropped from 7,400 fully funded graduate education programs during Vietnam to 396 for 2005, half of which are for Army's acquisition corps. (Killebrew, 2005)

The advantage technology can provide depends on the environment defining the battlespace. For example, the ability of technology to create a decisive advantage in irregular warfare in an urban environment is limited. As of 2001, 2.9 billion people, approximately half of the world's population, occupied urban areas. The number of urban areas will continue to increase over both the short term and the long term. It is estimated by 2030 that 3.9 billion people will live in cities, with the majority of growth occurring in under-developed regions of the world. (Fitzgerald, 2001) Technology must be developed to address the challenges of conducting combat operations in an urban environment: rapid breaching devices, IED identification and neutralization, protective equipment, powerful optics, and the ability to push down real-time imagery and intelligence to the tactical level. However, the more complex the urban environment, the more limited the advantage afforded by technology. The base line technology required is large numbers of well-trained infantrymen. (Grau, 1997) The man on the ground increases in importance in close combat where the enemy has be rooted out one or two at a time. Given the strategic trend of the increasing number of urban areas, the probability of fighting in urban environments will continue to increase in the future. Therefore, our force structure must address the demand for well-trained land forces with the right skill sets.

Force Structure

> "You can fly over a land forever; you may bomb it, atomize it, pulverize it and wipe it
> clean of life but if you desire to defend it, protect it, and keep it for civilization you must
> do this on the ground, the way the Roman Legions did, by putting your young men into
> the mud." (Fehrenbach et al, 1998)

Stability and support operations may be conducted concurrently or separately in the same theater during major combat operations. In fact, the proper application of a strategy of annihilation seeks to exploit simultaneity of operations to not only decisively defeat the enemies but also to deter potential enemies from pursuing policies or taking actions that are prejudicial to the vital interests of the United States.

Stability and support operations are predominately conducted in urban areas. Urban areas are key in establishing stability to include denying the enemy access to the local population and winning the information war. Urban warfare is complex because of its vertical dimensions and larger numbers of civilians in the battlespace. These civilians must not be turned into supporters of the insurgency, whether active or passive, or worse, insurgents during the execution of combat operations. Stability and support operations are not surgical or economy of force operations in nature. Even with technology, large numbers of troops are required to clear and control, or seize, small areas. Combat operations in an urban environment require military ground forces to both find and remove enemy forces by going door to door. Additionally, forces employed in an urban environment require a unique skill set derived from special close combat training. Applying constant pressure on the enemy requires these troops to be rotated for refit and backfilled by similar troops to retain the initiative.

Putting Soldiers and Marines on the ground is a political decision and requires political will. When United States land forces are put on the ground it is a symbol of a larger commitment of American of military forces. This psychological phenomenon has also permeated into the ranks of the United States' military members. Putting large numbers of land forces on the ground requires tremendous political will. A political decision to put a troop ceiling on the number of land forces to conduct a campaign is a decision to loose.

Joint Publication 3-07, Joint Doctrine for Military Operations Other Than War, states, "Commanders should remain aware of changes not only in the operational situation, but also of changes in political objectives that may warrant a change in military operations." (Joint Staff et al, 1995) Changes in political objectives may warrant not only a change in military operations, but may also warrant, if not require, a change in military strategy. The ability to rapidly change from one operational method to another operational method is referred to as flexibility. When not only the operational methods change, but also the mission, the ability to flex energy and resources is both increased in importance and more difficult. The combatant commander must have more than the mission tailored force, he must have sufficient operational forces and capabilities, to include reserves, to conduct decisive military operations throughout the joint operations area (JOA).

The American public's current resistance to deploying large numbers of military forces and the military's current force authorizations do not adequately address the combatant commander's requirements. Two simultaneous conflicts are a reality. Planners must have the intellectual agility to develop plans that reflect this reality. American military planners have done this well. However, intellectual agility has its limits. These same planners cannot indefinitely sustain commitments with no timeline for withdrawal given the current force authorization, operations tempo (OPTEMPO) and security environment. Resources are finite. Time cannot be regained and Service members, in an all volunteer force, cannot be retained when overtasked.

The 2001 *QDR* originally outlined the current 1-4-2-1 military force-sizing construct. The current *NDS* (2005) states the current force-sizing construct shapes and sizes the United States' military forces to do the following:

- (1) Defend the U.S. homeland;
- (4) Operate in and from four forward regions to assure allies and friends, dissuade competitors, and deter and counter aggression and coercion;
- (2) Swiftly Defeat adversaries in overlapping military campaigns; while
- (1) Preserving for the President the option to call for a more decisive and enduring result in one of the two conflicts.

At the same time, the armed forces must be ready to undertake a limited number of lesser contingency operations. Force structure must be able to achieve short-term and long-term warfighting success. The current force structure does not support the force-sizing construct. This is demonstrated by the temporary authorization of the Army and Marine Corps to exceed their end strength by 32,000 and 3,000 respectively.

The United States cannot know where the next war will be or who it will be against. Therefore, an expeditionary capable force is necessary. Expeditionary force is defined as an armed force organized to accomplish a specific objective in a foreign country. (Joint Staff et al, 2004) This definition is inadequate. In terms of mindset, an expeditionary force may be required to perform more than a single objective or the objective may change. More importantly, the term expeditionary is limiting in that it implies a limited force commitment of limited duration. This can partially be attributed to how Marines have historically been both employed and labeled expeditionary. These units typically deploy for short missions and have a limited sustainment capability.

The Department of Defense's goal is better interpreted as seeking a military with joint expeditionary capabilities, not a joint expeditionary force. The difference is one of both capabilities and mindset. Expeditionary capability has two requirements. First, strategic air and maritime lift assets must be available to provide the capability to rapidly project combat power anywhere in the world. Second, global basing of ground, sea air and space forces is required to minimize the lines of communication and the lines of operation required to rapidly project forces and employ those same forces anywhere in the world to reassure allies, deter, dissuade, and, if necessary, decisively defeat the enemies of the United States. Strategic lift and global basing are the basis for strategic maneuver.

Strategic maneuver is the ability to project military power rapidly from all points of the globe to converge simultaneously with overwhelming land, air, space, and maritime forces that paralyze and dominate the enemy. (Army Science Board) It enables America's joint military forces to get inside the OODA loop of its adversaries. A strategy of annihilation can further paralyze the enemy's ability to make strategic and operational decisions by affording the United States a psychological advantage which enables greater opportunities for diplomatic, informational and economic flexible deterrent options to be successful.

The United States is currently the world's only superpower, and with that is an associated cost for the United States. Nation states, no longer trapped in a bipolar world and the threat of mutually assured destruction, tend to walk along the fence rather than commit to supporting the policies of the United States. The recent history of the United Nations is testimony to this reality. Working through the United Nations is time consuming and can limit the ability of the United States to quickly act in the pursuit of its vital security interests. Furthermore, political and economic realities may impede the United Nations' ability to exercise definitive authority to coordinate international action.

Unilateral military action may be the only alternative; however, the United States should first always seek to build a "coalition of the willing" to increase the legitimacy of American actions in the international community. Given the choice between coalitions and alliances, the United States should always opt for coalition warfare. Alliances are harder because they are more rigid and well-defined by formal agreements. Coalitions are formed to address a specific crisis. The rules are developed as the crisis or operations progress. The major shareholder of resources makes the rules. The most important thing some countries bring to the fight is their flag; they are a unilateral action enabler. (Yeosock, 2005)

Other countries want the United States to bear the burden of policing the world. The end of the Cold War meant the elimination of the most powerful military threat to the Europe. With the exception of France, the majority of European countries spend less than two percent of their gross domestic product (GDP) on military defense. (Department of Defense, 2002) The level of commitment from many of these countries may be interpreted as they want to be involved, but not at the expense of costly military operations. These countries are more likely to contribute through the leveraging of their diplomatic, informational and economic elements of national power during the nation building phase of the operation.

Truly combined/joint operations may result in unhappy customers both internationally and nationally, especially when unlimited objectives are sought. This is true internationally because the United States will always be the main effort when the its vital national interests are involved, and if necessary will act unilaterally if international support is insufficient to mobilize a "coalition of the willing." Unhappy customers will also result nationally because unlimited objectives require the commitment of significant land forces which means the Reserve force, and possible the National Guard force, will be mobilized to support the Active Duty force. The bottom line is the United States cannot allow ideological opposition or emotional sentiment erode its political will act decisively. Washington's willingness to act without international support and, when necessary, against the wishes of all the American people further creates strategic paralysis for adversaries of the United States. Enemies of the United States will no longer be willing to test the resolve of the United States if the United States is consistent in both communicating its national objectives and then applying the necessary resources to secure those national objectives.

Windows, or gaps, are created by insufficient forces or capabilities. Windows of opportunity open and close rapidly during combat operations. The side that retains the initiative will continue to have these windows of opportunity to achieve objectives open rather than close. However, when they do open, forces must have enough structure to divert resources, retask and/or employ reserves. Diverting resources and retasking forces creates friction, but sufficient force structure minimizes friction. When military forces fail to exploit windows of opportunity and overcome friction they surrender the initiative and loose their ability to get inside the decision cycle of the enemy.

Combat operations are a destabilizing force. Combat operations to effect regime change create instability on a greater order of magnitude for the affected people. Stability operations are a challenge of scope, scale and size. The American military must be able to impose security and establish parameters to rapidly transition from major combat operations to reconstruction, or even conduct combat and reconstructions operations simultaneously. Security sets the conditions for government agencies and private organizations to assume not only an active, but a visible role in supporting operations.

Regardless of how large or small the footprint is, occupying troops are perceived as being oppressive. Military forces need to get in and get out as quickly as possible. However, they can only withdraw, or reposition in country, when the conditions for political and social change are established. This requires a substantial commitment of forces up front to facilitate the conditions for creating a local government, police, and military forces. The sooner the United States military is subordinated to American civil authorities in the occupied country the sooner it can begin to transition power to the developing host nation's civil government. Moreover, the sooner both United States civilian agencies and military forces are seen working side by side with local authorities the sooner tensions will begin to mitigate. This will further expedite the transition of responsibility to the new government and enables the joint force commander to merge the operational-level short-term effects of successful combat operations with the strategic-level long-term effects of regime change.

Conclusions and Recommendations

"You cannot qualify war in harsher terms than I will. War is cruelty, and you cannot refine it….and I will ever conduct war with a view to perfect and early success."
- General William T. Sherman in a letter to the mayor of Atlanta, September 12, 1864. (Sherman et al, 2000)

This paper discussed the necessity of nesting national and military strategy in order to match national and military objectives the strategic level. Neither is effective strategy if they are not coherent. Poor military strategy reduces national policy to a paper tiger. Conversely, vague national policy results in an ineffective national strategy, and, consequently, a directionless military strategy. Success begins at the top. Without definitive direction, service components cannot determine how to best man, train, and equip forces for future combat operations. Worse, service components may attempt to redefine themselves and stray from their warfighting competencies in an effort to be relevant. However, the nature of war has not changed. In fact, extremist organizations employing terror tactics have reinforced the need to employ overwhelming combat force throughout operations to not only destroy the extremists, but make an example of them.

Additionally, this study addressed adopting a military strategy of annihilation at the operational level as the nexus between linking grand national strategy and military strategy to achieve limited and unlimited objectives. Strategies of annihilation are resource intensive whether seeking limited or unlimited objectives. Achieving unlimited objectives demands tremendous resources, large land forces and a long-term commitment. Annihilation strategy is an asymmetric strategy that manages risks in the both short term and the long term. Overwhelming force enables the military to seize the initiative in the short-term and sustain momentum in the long-term by occupying the areas the enemy is conducting, or planning to conduct, operations. This overwhelming force must be systematically applied across the depth of the battlespace to attack enemy critical vulnerabilities to destroy enemy operational centers of gravity.

The "shock and awe" campaign of OIF, although it was extremely successful during major combat operations against the Iraqi conventional forces, failed to retain initiative, and thus the risks to American forces increased substantially during stability and support operations in urban areas to the point they were a gamble. The twenty-one day dash to Baghdad was a demonstration of speed, not momentum. Momentum is deliberate and coordinated. Speed is blind and uncoordinated. One official Army report stated, "The overly simplistic conception of the war led to a cascading undercutting of the war effort: too few troops, too little coordination with civilian and governmental/non-governmental agencies and too little time allotted to achieve success." (World Tribune.com, 2005) War is not the time to make a point about efficiency and effectiveness. In war quantity has a quality all its own.

The speed of the advance to Baghdad resulted in "catastrophic success." The rapid advance to Baghdad can partly be attributed to identifying the wrong Iraqi operational center of gravity. The real fight was in the Baghdad and surrounding cities, whether deliberately planned or not by Saddam, not in the open desert against a poorly lead and inadequately trained conventional Iraqi military. The resistance movement was most vulnerable at the end of major combat operations.

Casualties are inevitable in war. Credible strategy requires a demonstrated willingness to not only kill the enemy, but accept the reality of friendly casualties. National and military leadership cannot allow the fear of American casualties to result in employing a force that is not operationally effective. A sustained United States commitment of overwhelming military forces in the face of casualties will have the strategic effect of placing doubt in the mind of insurgent groups that they can be victorious. When the enemy's cognitive domain is pierced the military, and hence the nation, wins and begins to actually deter threats against the United States.

Technology is necessary, but it is neither a strategy nor a solution. An indigenous enemy will always have greater situational awareness without computers. Technology is helping the U.S. defeat IED's and reduce casualties; however, urban environments limit the effectiveness of technology. It is the Service member who must root out insurgents and make command decisions. During the Battle of Fallujah in November 2004, the Army and Marine forces were large enough to rotate forces and executed 72 hours of continuous combat operations to penetrate deep into the city. (Schmitt, 2004) Continuous operations of this nature throughout limited visibility were asymmetric in relation to the insurgents' capabilities. The constant pressure on the insurgents put them on the defensive and unable to regain the initiative. Precision munitions and artillery were not always able to root out insurgents from their defensive positions; sometimes they could not even be used due to potential collateral damage or civilian casualties. American military commanders employed armored bulldozers to bury the insurgents alive. (Ibid) As stated by General Sherman at the beginning of this section, "War is cruelty and you cannot refine it." Unlike the previous Fallujah offensive in April 2004, America's military sent a clear message to the insurgents.

The current force sizing construct is not supported by the current force as demonstrated by the over-dependence on Reserve forces to sustain operations in Afghanistan and Iraq. The significantly lower commitment of military forces in Afghanistan is critical to the efforts to stabilize Iraq. The reality is that current authorized end strength of the active duty force, specifically the Army as supported with Reserve and National Guard augmentation, could not support two operations on the scale of OIF to include the stability and support operations. This challenge is further exacerbated by inability of the Army, and the Marines on a lesser scale, to meet its recruitment goals for FY 05.

Private organizations as well as national and international organizations require a secure environment to operate. A strategy of annihilation sets the conditions for these entities as well as opening the channels for diplomatic, informational, and economic elements of national power to substantially contribute to the success of the operation. Collectively these efforts, though time intensive, are beginning to bear results. Beginning with the operational success in Afghanistan, an objective that eluded the Soviet Union for ten years, followed by the rebuilding the country, the United States sent a strategic message to its enemies and those who support them: the United States will not tolerate terrorism or other aggression against its national interests or its people.

Has the message been received? Yes. Look at the recent developments in Saudi Arabia, Lebanon and the Ukraine. In Saudi Arabia, a monarchy governed by Islamic law, the right of voting will be extended to women in the countries next municipal elections. Saudi Arabia has also been a voice in telling Syria to withdraw its military forces out of Lebanon. Amid pressure from the U.S government, the Saudi government and large-scale protests across the nation, Syria ended twenty-nine years of military occupation in Lebanon. The recent events in the Ukraine witnessed a population that would not stand for what it believed to be bogus initial election results, and were ultimately rewarded with the president the majority actually voted into office. The United States' commitment to make the world better, supported by its military forces in OEF and OIF, have served to steel other countries in the belief that regimes and oppression can be changed, and, if necessary, that America will force that change to make the world better.

Other indicators are also evident. In Iraq, reports indicate bomb-making skills dropping off and the current size of the insurgency is estimated by U.S. analysts to be around 16,000 strong as of April 2005, down 4,000 from its peek. (O'Hanlon, 2005) There are even signs the Anti-Iraqi Forces (AIF) are becoming desperate to undermine the efforts of the United States to build a free and self-determining Iraq. Evidence of this is the continuing increase of attacks against Iraqi civilians resulting in Iraqis openly fighting back against the insurgents. These actions actually work to undermine passive, and potentially active, support for the insurgents and reduce their operational center of gravity while enlarging the support of the Iraqi people – the strategic center of gravity – for social and political reform. Recent polls also indicate 62% of Iraqis believe Iraq is headed in the right direction. (Slavin, 2005) Most recently, a captured letter indicated the constant pressure on the AIF had resulted in uncoordinated operations, low morale, and an increased potential for members of the organization to turn in key leaders for monetary rewards. (Scarborough, 2005)

The November offensive in Fallujah was a watershed event for the United States in OIF. The continuing commitment since that time to keep constant pressure on the insurgents regardless of adverse regional media coverage or threats of violence has began to yield positive results. Arguably Iraq would be more stable if the American led Coalition had been able to sustain a more aggressive posture immediately following the fall of Baghdad.

The United States cannot declare victory in Iraq yet. Fallujah is but one intermediate operational objective in the GWOT. The United States must still address the challenges of the future security environment beginning with expanding and restructuring the current military force. The current force was created following the Gulf War in 1991. The threat has changed, but the force to meet that threat has not. Raising the maximum age for individuals to enter Reserve military service to thirty-nine years old and cutting back professional military education during the current OPTEMPO are not solutions.

The United States must be unequivocally willing to act alone in order to deter current or potential enemies. Major combat operations over space and time require large numbers of boots on the ground. Combat operations in the enemy's urban areas are manpower intensive and inevitable. Securing lines of communication in a non-contiguous battlefield further increases the requirement for boots on the ground. More ground forces will be needed to conduct stability and support operations. This reality is not new to combat operations; however, infantrymen compromise only about 6% of the total military. (Scales, 2005)

Studies from British peacekeeping operations in Northern Ireland concluded that a security forces require "…a ratio of about 20 per thousand inhabitants." (Quinlivan, 2005) Northern Ireland and England share a common language and culture. In Iraq, a country of twenty-five million people, that equates to a minimum 500,000 troops to conduct the military occupation. (Ibid) In theory, this number could be much higher given the language and cultural barriers that exists between Iraq and the United States.

Proponents for increasing the size of land components recommend increasing the Army's ground forces by 150,000 over the next four years as well as adding two more Marine Expeditionary Brigades (MEB). (Scales, 2005) Filling the billets is an entirely separate issue for authorizing the billets. Building combat units takes time. In addition to recruiting more soldiers, a professional cadre is required for raw recruits to fall in on. Assuming recruitment is not an obstacle, it still requires about three years to train and equip an effective fighting force from ground zero. Again, the problem is one of short planning horizons. Expanding the military is a strategic decision, not a tactical action.

An expanded military can support a military strategy of annihilation, which in turn best supports national objectives of the United States and the welfare of its citizens. However, it must have the support of the American populous. National leaders must establish unambiguous objectives. Military leaders must be empowered to employ decisive military force to achieve the military objectives required to secure national objectives. Any potential for enemy victory must be replaced by the certainty of rapid defeat when threatening the vital interests of America and its people. The introduction of a paradigm focused on clear objectives and decisive victories by applying overwhelming force will create conditions that limit casualties and the drain on national resources in the long-term both operationally and strategically. Only then will the United States begin to win the GWOT and secure the peace.

Bibliography

Army Takes Over in Capital. (2003). Retrieved Apr. 22, 2005, from http://www.jsonline.com/news/gen/apr03/135092.asp?format=print.

BrainyQuotes. (n.d.). Retrieved Feb. 26, 2005, from Dwight D. Eisenhower Quotes Web site: http://www.brainyquote.com/quotes/quotes/d/dwightdei124835.html.

Cave, D. (2005). Army Recruiters Say They Feel Pressure to Bend Rules. *New York Times*. Retrieved May 4, 2005, from Early Bird Web site: http://ebird.afis.osd.mil/ebfiles/e20050503366409.

Clausewitz, K. (1993). *On War*. New York: Everyman's Library.

Coalition Casualty Count: Metrics. (2005). Retrieved Mar. 03, 2005, from http://icasualties.org/oif/Stats.aspx

Collins, J. (2003). You Can't Assume Nothin'. Retrieved Apr. 21, 2005, from Proceedings Magazine Web site: http://www.usni.org/proceedings/Articles03/PROcollins05.htm.

Defense Link News. (2001). Retrieved Apr. 18, 2005, from American Forces Information Service Web site: http://www.dod.gov/news/Feb2001/n02272001_200102271.html.

Department of Defense. (2002). Allied Contributions to the Common Defense. Retrieved May 4, 2005, from Web site: http://www.defenselink.mil/pubs/allied_contrib2002/index.html.

Dunham, W. (2005). Amid War, U.S. Army, Marines Miss Recruiting Goals. Retrieved from Reuters Foundation Web site: http://www.alertnet.org/printable.htm?URL=?thenews/newsdesk/N01360669.htm.

Enabling Rapid and Decisive Strategic Maneuver for the Army after 2010. (n.d.). Retrieved Apr. 13, 2005, from http://www.dtic.mil/ndia/cannon/fisch.pdf.

Faust, P. (Ed). (2002). Cost of The American Civil War. Retrieved Mar. 21, 2005, from http://www.civilwarhome.com/warcosts.htm.

Fehrenbach, T. (1998). *This Kind of War:The Classic Korean War History*. Dulles, VA: Brassey.

Female Fatalities. (2005). Retrieved Mar. 22, 2005, from http://icasualties.org/oif/female.aspx.

Female Personnel by Service. (1999). Retrieved Mar. 21, 2005, from Military Casualty Information Web site: http://www.dior.whs.mil/mmid/casualty/wft.pdf.

Fitzgerald, C. (2001). The Changing the Face of Urban Warfare. *Armed Forces Journal*. February 2001, 18 – 19.

Franks, T. (2004). *American Soldier*. New York: Harper-Collins.

Gaddis, J. (2003). Frontline. Retrieved Nov. 06, 2004, from Interview: John Lewis Gaddis Web site: http://www.pbs.org/wgbh/pages/frontline/shows/iraq/interviews/gaddis.html.

Gaddis, J. (2004). *Surprise, Security, and the American Experience*. Cambridge, MA: Harvard University Press.

Grant, U. (1990). *Grant: Memoirs and Selected Letters*. New York: Literary Classics of the United States, Inc.

Grau, L. (1997). Bashing the Laser Range Finder with a Rock . Retrieved Jan. 1, 2005, from http://www.geocities.com/Hollywood/Set/7906/graunew.htm.

Griess, T. (Ed.). (1986). *The West Point Military History Series: Atlas for the American Civil War*. Wayne, NJ: Avery Publishing Group, Inc.

Griess, T. (Ed.). (2002). *The West Point Military History Series: The American Civil War*. Grand City Park, New York: Square One Publishers.

Hart, L. (1991). *Strategy*. New York: Meridian.

Helmly, J. (2004). Readiness of the United States Army Reserve. Retrieved Feb. 15, 2005, from Web site: http://www.baltimoresun.com/media/acrobat/2005-01/15715020.pdf

Iraq. (2005). Retrieved Apr. 30, 2005, from CIA - The World Fact Book Web site: http://www.cia.gov/cia/publications/factbook/geos/iz.html.

Joint Staff. (2004). *Joint Publication 1-02, Department of Defense Dictionary of Military and Associated Terms*. Department of Defense.

Joint Staff. (2004). *Joint Publication 3-0, Doctrine for Joint Operations*. Department of Defense.

Joint Staff. (1995). *Joint Publication 3-07, Joint Doctrine for Military Operations Other Than War*. Department of Defense.

Joint Staff. (1995). *Joint Publication 3-11, Joint Doctrine for Nuclear, Biological, and Chemical (NBC) Defense*. Department of Defense.

Joint Staff. (1993). *Joint Publication 3-12, Joint Doctrine for Nuclear Operations*. Department of Defense.

Kaplan, R. (2002). *Warrior Politics: Why Leadership Demands a Pagan Ethos*. New York: Random House, Inc..

Killebrew, R. (2005). Winning Wars. Retrieved Apr. 29, 2005, from Army Magazine Web site: http://www.ausa.org/pdfdocs/RBKillebrew.pdf.

Klinger, J. (2002). Commentary and Reply. *Parameters, US Army War College Quarterly*, (3), 129.

Knickerbocker, B. (2003). Pentagon's Quietest Calculation: The Casualty Count. Retrieved Mar. 22, 2005, from GlobalSecurity.org Web site: http://www.globalsecurity.org/org/news/2003/030127-casualties01.htm.

Lincoln, A. (1863). General Orders No. 100. Retrieved Apr. 4, 2005, from Laughter Genealogy Web Site: http://www.laughtergenealogy.com/bin/histprof/misc/genord100.html.

Metz, S. and Johnson D. (2001). Asymmetry and U.S. Military Strategy: Definition, Background, and Strategic Concepts. Retrieved Nov. 10, 2004, from http://www.au.af.mil/au/awc/awcgate/ssi/asymetry.pdf.

Moniz, D. (2005, Mar 3). Army Misses Recruiting Goal. *USA Today*, p. 9.

Myers, R. (2003). The New American Way of War. Retrieved Feb. 16, 2005, from http://www.usafa.af.mil/dfps/meyersEaker2003.htm.

National Defense Strategy of The United States of America. (2005).

National Military Strategy of The United States of America. (2004).

National Security Strategy of The United States of America. (2002).

O'Hanlon, M., and de Albuquerque, A. (2005). Iraq Index. Retrieved Apr. 30, 2005, from Brookings Institution Web site: http://www.brookings.edu/dybdocroot/fp/saban/iraq/index.pdf.

Quadrennial Defense Review Report. (1997).

Quadrennial Defense Review Report. (2001).

Quinlivan, J. (2005). Burden of Victory: The Painful Arithmetic of Stability Operations. Retrieved Feb. 23, 2005, from Rand Web site: http://www.rand.org/publications/randreview/issues/summer2003/burden.html.

Operation Enduring Freedom - Casualty Summary by Type. (2005). Retrieved Mar. 21, 2005, from Military Casualty Information Web site: http://www.dior.whs.mil/mmid/CASUALTY/WOTSUM.PDF.

Persian Gulf War - Casualty Summary. (2004). Retrieved Mar. 21, 2005, from Military Casualty Information Web site: http://www.dior.whs.mil/mmid/casualty/dstorm.pdf.

Peters, R. (2005). A Grave New World. *Armed Forces Journal*, Retrieved Apr 2005, from Web site: http://ebird.afis.osd.mil/ebfiles/e20050405361625.html.

Peters, R. (2004). In Praise of Attrition. *Paramters: US Army War College Quarterly*, (2), 24 - 32.

Peters, R. (2002). In War Soldiers Die. *The Wall Street Journal*. Retrieved Mar 22, 2005, from Web site: http://www.opinionjournal.com/editorial/feature.html?id=105001725

Principle Wars in which the United States Participated. (2003). Retrieved Mar. 22, 2005, from Military Casualty Information Web site: http://web1.whs.osd.mil/mmid/casualty/WCPRINCIPAL.pdf.

Pike, J. (2005). Iraqi Insurgency Groups. Retrieved Apr. 30, 2005, from Iraqi Insurgency Web site: http://www.globalsecurity.org/military/ops/iraq_insurgency.htm.

Project on Defense Alternatives. (2004). Mobilized US National Guard and Reserve, Oct 2001 – Sep 2004. Retrieved in Jan. 2005, from Web site: http://www.comw.org/pda/fulltext/041019Guard&Reserve.pdf.

Rascon, C. (n.d.) The Civil War, Part 1: 1861-1865. Retrieved Apr. 5, 2005, from: http://w3fp.arizona.edu/nrotc/310/14.ppt.

Rosenberg, C. (2003). Delaware's Dover Air Force Base Receives and Honors America's Fallen Soldiers. *Detroit Free Press*. Retrieved Mar 3, 2005, from http://www.freep.com/cgi-bin/forms/printerfriendly.pl

Scales, R. (2005, Jan 25). Ground Forces Too Small. *Washington Times*, p. 17.

Schmitt, E., and Shanker, T. (2004) Past Battles Won and Lost Helped In Fallujah Assault. *New York Times*. Retrieved Nov. 11, 2004, from http://ebird.afis.osd.mil/ebfiles/e20041122338960.html.

Schmitt, E. (2005). Marines Come up Short on Recruits. *New York Times*. Retrieved Mar 03, 2005, from http://www.sfgate.com/cgi-bin/article.cgi?file=/c/a/2005/02/03/MNGM2B50V61.DTL

Smith, R. (n.d.). Retrieved Mar. 14, 2005, from Casualties - US vs NVA/VC Web site: http://www.rjsmith.com/kia_tbl.html.

Scarborough, R. (2005). Letter Reveals Terror Group's Woes in Iraq. *The Washington Times*. Retrieved May 4, 2005, from Early Bird Web site: http://ebird.afis.osd.mil/ebfiles/e20050504366535.html.

Selected Military Operations . (2003). Retrieved Mar. 22, 2005, from Military Casualty Information Web site: http://web1.whs.osd.mil/mmid/casualty/table13.htm.

Sherman, W. (2000). *Memoirs of General W.T. Sherman.* New York: Penguin Books.

Sir Basil Henry Liddel-Hart. (n.d.). Retrieved Feb. 26, 2005, from Military Quotes.com Web site: http://www.military-quotes.com/Liddelhart.htm.

Slavin, B. (2005). Most Iraqis Say Future Looks Brighter. USA Today. Retrieved Mar. 16, 2005, from Early Bird Web site: http://ebird.afis.osd.mil/ebfiles/e20050316357789.html.

Smith, R. (2000). Retrieved Mar. 21, 2005, from Casualties- US vs NVA/VC Web site: http://www.rjsmith.com/kia_tbl.html.

Strange, J. and Iron, R. (n.d.). *Understanding Centers of Gravity and Critical Vulnerabilities.* JAWS Seminar Handout.

Strange, J. (1998). *Perspectives on Warfighting: Capital "W" War.* 6th ed. Quantico, VA: Marine Corps University.

Stanton, S. (1985). *The Rise and Fall of the American Army: U.S. Ground Forces in Vietnam, 1965 - 1973.* New York: Presidio Press.

Summers, H. (1984). *On Strategy: A Critical Analysis of the Vietnam War.* New York: Dell Publishing.

USA Today. (2005). Army and Marines Fall Short of Recruiting Goals. Retrieved May 4, 2005, from Early Bird Web Site: http://ebird.afis.osd/mil/ebfiles/e20050503366399.html.

USMC Combat Development Command. (1997). *Marine Corps Doctrinal Publication 1-1, Strategy.* U.S. Marine Corps.

USMC Combat Development Command. (1997). *Marine Corps Doctrinal Publication 1-2, Campaigning.* U.S. Marine Corps.

Vego, M. (2000). Operational Overreach and the Culmination Point. *Joint Force Quarterly,* (25), 99 - 106.

Vietnam Conflict - Casualty Summary. (2002). Retrieved Mar. 21, 2005, from Military Casualty Information Web site: http://www.dior.whs.mil/mmid/CASUALTY/vietnam.pdf.

Weigley, R. (1973). *The American Way of War: A History of United States Military Strategy and Policy.* Indianapolis, IN: Indian University Press.

World Trade Center New York Destruction. (n.d.). Retrieved Mar. 15, 2005, from http://www.solcomhouse.com/Worldtradecenter.htm.

World Tribune.com. (2005). Army Report: U.S. Lost Control in Iraq Three Months After Invasion. Retrieved Mar. 21, 2005, from http://216.26.163.62/2005/ss_iraq_03_07.html.

Yeosock, J. (2005, Jan 07). *The Persian Gulf War.* Lecture at the Joint Forces Staff College, Norfolk, VA.

Map B: General Grant's Operations in the Eastern Theater

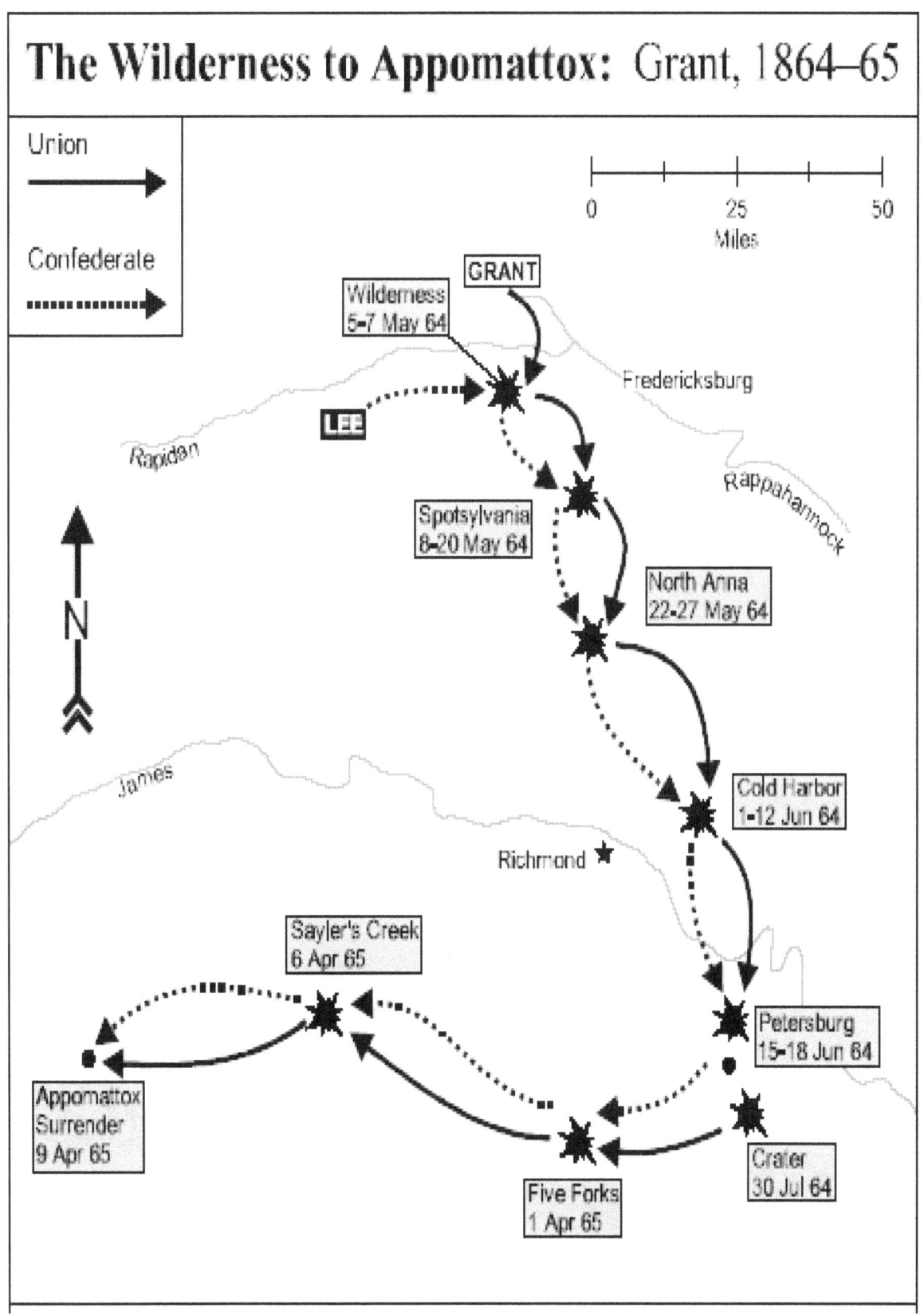

The Wilderness to Appomattox: Grant, 1864–65

From MCDP 1-2. (Marine Corps Doctrine Command, 1997)

www.ingramcontent.com/pod-product-compliance
Lightning Source LLC
Chambersburg PA
CBHW081328310526
45789CB00018B/2574